QUILTING with Stash or Cash

10 Patterns, 20 Quilts, Lots of Creative Options

Linda J. Hahn and Deborah G. Stanley

Landauer Publishing

Acknowledgments

We'd like to thank our Stashers for this book—Stevii Graves, Linda Hallatt, Amy Chaney, Carmen Solomon, Rebecca Szabo, Anne-Marie Neumann, Daria Eisen, and Levi Henson. It was so much fun to see your interpretations!

A HUGE thank-you to Banyan Batiks, Northcott Silk, and Hoffman California for sharing your gorgeous fabrics.

Thank-you to our editor Amelia Johanson and the entire team at Fox Chapel Publishing. What beautiful books you produce for us!

Quilting with Stash or Cash

Landauer Publishing, www.landauerpub.com, is an imprint of Fox Chapel Publishing Company, Inc.

Copyright © 2021 by Linda J. Hahn, Deborah G. Stanley, and Fox Chapel Publishing Company, Inc., 903 Square Street, Mount Joy, PA 17552.

ISBN 978-1-947163-65-2

Library of Congress Control Number: 2021939136

We are always looking for talented authors. To submit an idea, please send a brief inquiry to acquisitions@foxchapelpublishing.com.

Printed in the United States of America
24 23 22 21   2 4 6 8 10 9 7 5 3 1

Introduction

The Stash or Cash Concept

While we all love to handle and buy new fabric, the current economy (and the COVID-19 pandemic, which is occurring at the time of writing) has inspired many quilters to delve into their stash to find fabric for their projects. With the Cash or Stash concept, we want to show you how to easily create a quilt using purchased fabric (Cash), as well as how you can adapt the project to use what you have in your home supply right now (Stash).

Each project in this book is presented in two different ways: Cash or Stash. Note that some of the piecing methods for the quilts are different; we will explore those.

First, let's define the types of quilts that you will find in this book.

- **Cash quilts:** Are made with a defined amount of yardage so that you can go into a quilt shop, choose your fabrics, and use quick piecing techniques (such as strip piecing, Triangles on a Roll, etc.) to make the project. The fabric may be in yardage (meters) or available in a precut package.
- **Stash quilts:** Are made using what you currently have in your stash, which could also include fabric or pieces from your scrap basket. You may be required to use similar colors or similar fabrics to use them up, and you might also need to substitute a piece or two to make the color scheme work. You will actually feel a sense of accomplishment going through and cutting up your stash and scraps.
- **Scrap quilts:** Scrap quilts are made from scraps. There may just be one small piece of a particular fabric or color or there may be "just enough" to do one block. There could also be a combination of stash and scraps.

The Challenge

We decided to base the concept of this book on a challenge. We, the authors, designed the Cash quilts in this book. We then provided our Stash designers with our Cash quilt images and patterns and asked them to make the same quilt using **only** what they had in their stashes. They were not allowed to purchase any fabric, so they had to use up their stash, make do, or do without.

We did **not** see any of their fabric choices ahead of time, **nor** did we see the quilts until they arrived at our door. It was so exciting and thrilling to see how each of the Stash designers interpreted the instructions and the designs to use what they had to make their assigned quilts.

The Stash designers did have some leeway, especially when it came down to border options. Some used scraps, some used larger pieces from their stash, some had to substitute fabrics after running out of what they were using, and some had to think creatively when it was time to add the borders.

Not only were we pleased with the results, we're also happy to use this challenge to show our readers the versatility of these quilt designs. We know that you can make your own unique quilt whether you decide to buy new fabric or use up your stash pile.

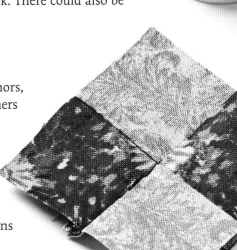

Contents

18

42

66

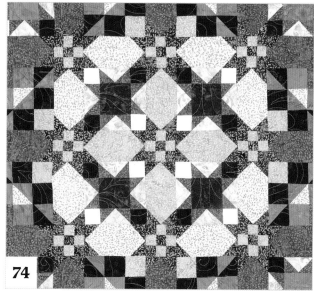

74

Materials

Scrap Management

There are many, many different ways that quilters manage their scraps: by size, by color, or just "dumped."

BY SIZE

Sorting by size is fairly popular. To sort in this way, you need to determine what fabric piece sizes you usually use for your quilts, then store them by size in labeled boxes or bins. As you gain scraps from finished projects, just cut them into whatever sizes you need and place them into the designated box. Here are a few examples of typical sizes:

- 2½" (6.35cm) squares or strips
- 4½" (11.43cm) squares (can be matched with 2½" [6.35cm] squares)
- 2½" x 4½" (6.35 x 11.43cm) rectangles
- Everything else goes into a separate container to use for English Paper Piecing projects (of a predetermined size).

BY COLOR

This one is pretty self-explanatory. Simply organize all of your fabrics according to color. This method makes it easier to find specific colors needed for your Stash quilts.

BY DUMPING

Choose a pretty basket or bin to toss all of your scraps in without cutting them into predetermined sizes. Make a promise to yourself that when the basket is full, you will make a scrap quilt, or at the very least, some quilt blocks.

To make quilts or blocks with fabrics stored this way, simply dump the basket onto your table and start cutting the scraps into the sizes you will need.

You will need to determine the size of the smallest scrap you are willing to keep. You can make a separate container for those pieces. Find someone in your group or guild that uses scraps for pet beds or does a lot of appliqué. This way you won't feel like you are throwing something out—you are just repurposing that fabric.

No Stash . . . No Problem

Some quilters buy their fabrics on a project-by-project basis. That said, quilters love their fabrics, and they can accumulate a stash rather quickly. If you've recently gotten into quilting, however, you probably don't have much of a stash. Precuts are a great way to get started!

Different manufacturers have different names for the variety of offerings. Here are just a few examples:

- 2½" (6.35cm) strips
  - Hoffman Fabrics Bali Pops™
  - Hoffman Fabrics Bali Poppies™
  - Timeless Treasures Tonga Treats™
  - Jelly rolls (from various brands)
- 10" (10.4cm) square packs
  - Hoffman Bali Crackers
  - Layer cakes (from various brands)

You can also purchase fabric bundles. These can usually be found in 18" x 22" (45.7 x 56cm) fat-quarter cuts in coordinated colors/fabrics from a specific collection or perhaps color gradations.

How Much Fabric to Buy?

The amount of fabric to buy is up to the individual quilter. For a 72" x 90" (183 x 228.6cm) twin-size quilt, you might buy 3 yards (2.7m) of a certain fabric if you think it might work well for a border. If there is a cute novelty fabric that might work for a backing, then perhaps you would need to purchase 5–6 yards (4.6-5.5m). If you tend to make larger quilts—like a 90" x 108" (228.6 x 274.3cm) queen-size or 120" (305cm) square king-size blanket—you may wish to increase the border fabric to 4 yards (3.7m) and the backing to 9 yards (8.2m).

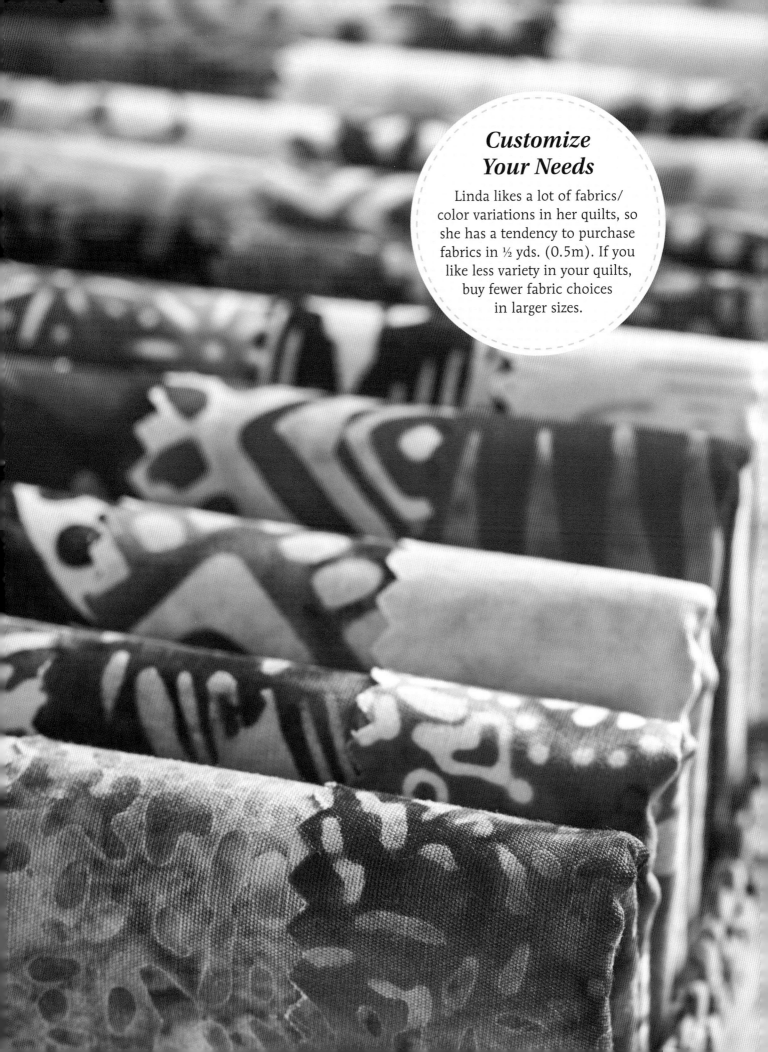

Customize Your Needs

Linda likes a lot of fabrics/ color variations in her quilts, so she has a tendency to purchase fabrics in ½ yds. (0.5m). If you like less variety in your quilts, buy fewer fabric choices in larger sizes.

Tools

Quilters have all sorts of different preferences when it comes to the tools they favor. Some stick with the basics; others try out every new notion that comes on the market. We tend to fall somewhere in between, relying on our favorites to get the job done, but not afraid to try out something new. Detailed here are the tools we used to help us make the quilts in this book.

Rulers

We always use the the same brand of ruler, if possible; we find it's best for size and marking consistency. Look for a long ruler for cutting strips and a square ruler for squaring blocks. We use Omingrid® brand rulers. Our favorite of all time is the 9½" (24.1cm) square ruler; it fits perfectly in your hand. The 6" x 24" (15.2 x 61cm) is ideal for cutting strips.

Rotary Cutters

Rotary cutters are available in small (helpful for small areas and curves), medium (for general use) and large (for cutting multiple layers) sizes. We don't use a fancy or ergonomic cutter—just a plain, straightedge cutter in the medium size. We like the Olfa® 45mm. For accurate cutting, you need a nice, sharp blade, so change your blades often. For safety, always engage the blade cover or retractor when not in use.

With a few basic tools you can make any quilt in this book. A cutting mat, rotary cutter, and ruler are the most essential.

Cutting Mats

Only cut on a specialized mat designed for use with a rotary cutter. These self-healing mats come in a variety of sizes. A 36" (91.4cm) mat is ideal, the larger the mat the better for general work.

Seam Ripper

Seam rippers, which insert in the seam to slice through the thread line, are essential to any quilting project. Like rotary blades, keeping a fresh sharp seam ripper on hand makes sure your threads are cut easily and don't pull the fabric out of line.

Threads

Using the proper thread can mean the difference between frustration and success in piecing and quilting. Choose a good quality cotton thread and use the same type of thread in the machine and in the bobbin. We use and recommend neutral colors from AurifilTM 50 wt. on top and in bobbin for piecing. Beige, taupe, or light gray are our favorite colors. Never use metallic thread, quilting thread or very old thread for piecing.

Pins

Sharp, heat-resistant pins are important for quilting as you'll be pressing throughout the process. The quilting variety is longer and stronger than typical dressmaking pins. If layering for machine quilting, use basting pins, which are a curved safety pin made specifically for quilting to secure your layers.

Marking Tools

We always work with chalk-based marking tools; they are easier to work with and recommend the Clover Chaco-Liner. If you're opting for marking pens, always test them on your fabric to determine both the ease at which it marks the fabric, and to make sure it can be removed easily.

Needles

We use a 90/14 Topstitch needle for everything. This needle has a large eye and a sharp point. You can also use this needle for quilting as it will accommodate a variety of thread weights— even metallic!

Piecing Guide

The What's My Angle tool is a seam guide you can tape directly to your machine and use over and over. It aids in making connector squares super quickly without having to mark your fabric, and you can use it to make Flying Geese, diagonal corners and ends, triangle squares and mitered corners.

Half-Square Triangle Paper

When we have to make a lot of half-square triangles, we will use Triangles on a Roll, which is a paper grid for sewing and cutting. These papers help move things along more quickly.

Pressing Board

We use the Steady Betty® Pressing Board when piecing quilts. It's just the right size to go next to your sewing machine.

Spray Starch

We prefer to starch our fabrics prior to cutting, and then also during the stitching process. Niagara® Pump Spray, which allows you to really direct a concentrated stream at a seam or crease is our favorite.

Batting

Batting is available in a variety of different sizes and qualities. A 100% cotton batting offers a more vintage look. A polyester blend creates a smoother, less-wrinkled finish. Batting comes in bolts to be cut to size or in packages.

Learn the Lingo

Before you begin, please read through the following definitions of the various terms and abbreviations that we will be using throughout this book.

- **WOF –** This is an abbreviation for "width of fabric." It means selvedge to selvedge, usually 40–42" (101.6–106.7cm) of usable fabric.
- **HST –** An abbreviation for "half-square triangle."
- **Connector –** This is the term used to describe the method of stitching a square on the diagonal and folding over to create a triangle on a larger square/rectangle. Sometimes called "snowball corners."
- **Connector square –** The smaller square that is stitched onto the base of a block to connect it to another.
- **Base –** The larger square or rectangle that the connector is stitched to.

- **Crosscut –** The method of cutting fabric (usually used in strip piecing) into smaller units after stitching. Sometimes called "sub-cut."
- **Cash quilts –** Quilts made from a defined amount of purchased yardage (as if you were following a pattern).
- **Stash quilts –** Quilts made from what you have in your fabric supply *right now*—it could be fat quarters, ½ yards (0.5m), or larger pieces.
- **Scraps –** For our purposes, anything smaller than a fat quarter.
- **RST –** The abbreviation for "right sides together."
- **RSU –** The abbreviation for "right side up."
- **RSD –** The abbreviation for "right side down."
- **Scant ¼" (0.6cm) –** A few threads less than a ¼" (0.6cm) seam.

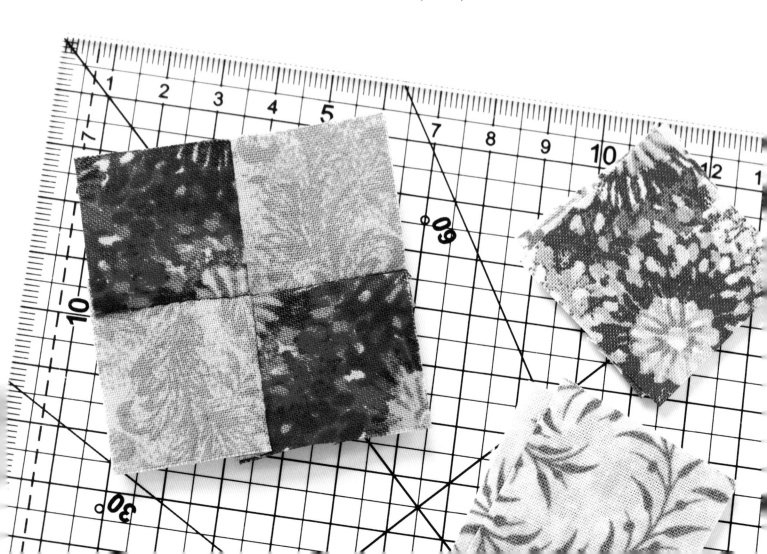

Techniques

Half-square Triangles

There are several different ways to make a half-square triangle (HST). We prefer the traditional method described in this section, but you may like another better. Try them all and choose the method that works best for you.

TRADITIONAL TECHNIQUE

When using the traditional method, do not use measurements with ⅞" (2.2cm); rather, round up by ⅛" (0.3cm) and work with whole numbers. For example, if you wish the HST to be 2" (5.1cm) finished, cut the squares 3" (7.6cm) so they're 1" (2.5cm) larger than the desired finished size.

1 With the fabric squares right side together (RST), draw a diagonal line from corner to corner.

2 Stitch a scant ¼" (0.6cm) on each side of the drawn line.

3 Cut on the drawn line to create two HSTs.

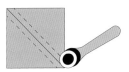

4 Trim to the desired unfinished size by placing the diagonal line on the ruler in the seam allowance (which equally distributes the fabric on both sides).

LIMITED FABRIC TECHNIQUE

As indicated previously, we like the traditional HST method, but there may be a time when you don't have a pair of squares or strips in the larger size. You *can* still get the needed HSTs using squares cut using the unfinished size; however, there will be some waste involved.

1 If you need a 2½" (6.4cm) square unfinished HST and do not have enough fabric for 3" (7.6cm) squares, you can take a pair of the required fabrics cut into 2½" (6.4cm) squares. Draw a diagonal line from corner to corner.

2 Stitch on the diagonal line.

3 Fold back one of the triangles and trim away the fabrics underneath. The cutaways are waste.

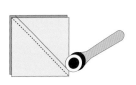

Tips for Using Triangles on a Roll

- Work with a width of fabric (WOF) cut in half if at all possible. It is just easier to manipulate under the sewing machine.
- Extend the fabric slightly beyond the paper so there is something to hold on to when stitching. Add an extra ½" (1.3cm) to the recommended WOF on the TOAR paper.
- Place the fabric that you are pressing toward right side up (RSU) on the bottom and the fabric you are pressing away from right side down (RSD).
- Spritz with starch and press the two fabrics together.

PAPER TECHNIQUE

Our favorite way of making HSTs with the paper technique is by using a product called Triangles on a Roll™ (TOAR). You must purchase them by the finished size that you wish your HST to be. We use them slightly different than as described in the directions on the package.

1 Roll out the paper and pin securely.

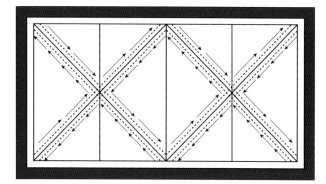

2 Stitch following the arrows on the paper.

3 When you have completed stitching, press on the wrong side.

4 Use a rotary cutter and a cutting mat to cut into two pieces on the drawn lines.

5 Place the triangles paper side down on an ironing board. One by one, take each and press them closed and then press open WITH the paper ON. Leaving the paper on provides a little more stability.

6 Clip the bunny ears and remove the paper. Your perfect triangles are now good to go!

FABRIC STRIP TECHNIQUE

If your fabric is large enough for triangles but too small for squares, no problem. Follow this technique to make HSTs without squares.

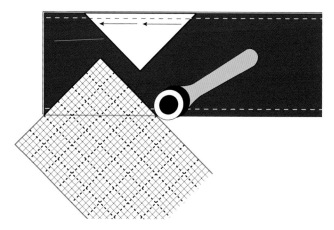

1 Draw out the triangle's measurements on a piece of paper and cut it apart. (You can also cut off a section from the TOAR for this step as well.)

2 Measure from the edge to the point. Add ¼–½" (0.6–1.3cm) to that measurement for the seam allowance if you'd like.

3 Stitch two strips (yes, strips) along the long side that have been cut the width of your measurement, plus the seam allowance measurements.

4 Place the triangle on the strip, matching the seam allowance on the paper to that on the stitched strip.

5 Place the ruler over the triangle and cut. Note the marks on the ruler so that you can place it down on the other triangle. If it helps, you can also tape the triangle on the back of the ruler.

Strip Piecing

You may think that strip piecing is really easy—just place two strips together and stitch along the long side. However, some quilters may encounter frustration during the strip-piecing process, resulting in wonky/wavy strips. We have some suggestions to keep your strips straight. To begin, starching will definitely help!

The first thing we suggest is tearing your fabric to put it on the straight of grain. Tearing is not suggested for fabrics with a low thread count as you may just make a mess, but it's fine to tear a batik or tightly woven fabric.

Starch and press each fabric. We like to layer cut the strips by placing them on top of each other lining up the torn edges. Cut your strips by WOF. Then cut those in half so that you are working with 20–21" (50.8–53.3cm) strips, rather than the whole WOF. The smaller size is so much easier to work with and less likely to wave.

Stitch with the fabric you are pressing toward on the top using a ¼" (0.6cm) seam allowance. Don't stretch the strips, but rather let the feed dogs do their work and move the strips along under the needle.

1 With right sides together, stitch the starched strips. Press closed.

2 Open up the strip and place the tip of the iron just to the right of the seam (in the ditch).

3 Lift the strip at an angle as you glide the tip of the iron along the ditch.

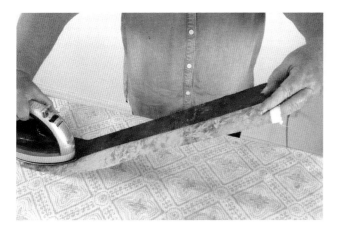

4 Lay the strip set back flat and spritz once again with starch. Press the strip set open, again with the point of the iron in the ditch.

5 Now that your strip sets are cut and pressed, you can save some time by layer cutting the strip set. Place the strip sets RST. Using your fingers, gently interlock the seams.

6 Trim the edge and then cut the strips into the required size. The pieces are already interlocked, and you can stack them next to your machine ready to piece.

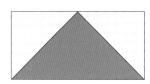

Connector Squares

This technique, made famous by the late Mary Ellen Hopkins, is an easy way to get the look of a triangle without having to cut on the bias and attempt to accurately stitch on a triangle. We use this method throughout this book! The "connector" fabric is the square that you are placing onto the "base" fabric. Connectors can be applied to squares or strips.

1 Draw a diagonal line from corner to corner on the connector square with an erasable marking device.

2 Place the connector square on top of the base RST, paying attention to the direction of the drawn line. Stitch ON the drawn line from corner to corner.

3 Cut away the bottom two fabrics approximately ¼" (0.6cm) from the stitched line. Fold the triangle flat and press.

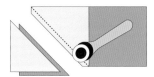 

4 Repeat on the opposite side. There will be a slight overlap of the second connector square.

5 Press your pieces. Starch if you like.

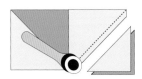 

STITCH DIRECTION MATTERS

The direction of the stitching on the connector square can create a variety of options:

Flying Geese Unit

Chevron Units

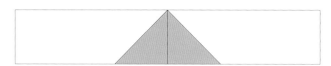

Triangle in the Center of Rectangle

Square in a Square

Adding Borders

You worked hard on your blocks and are probably anxious to finish the top so you can start quilting. *Please do NOT rush to finish by adding the borders without measuring them. As long arm quilters, we have seen many beautiful quilts distorted when the borders are attached without taking the time to measure and attach them properly.*

Sometimes the size of your quilt can change by the time you reach the final stage of adding borders. This change can occur because of all of the seams involved in piecework. For this reason, it is a good idea to cut the borders to the size of your actual quilt—not necessarily to the instructions of the pattern that you are using. We always cut the borders *after* piecing the inside of the top.

> ### Size differences can be the result of inconsistent seam allowances or pressing techniques.

When possible, we prefer to cut borders along the straight of grain, which is parallel to the selvage edge, rather than the cross grain. We also tear off the selvage before cutting as this edge is a much tighter weave and sometimes has printing on it.

PIECING BORDER/SASHING STRIPS

When piecing a border or sashing strips, we recommend using a diagonal seam instead of a straight seam. Diagonal seams help distribute the bulk of the seams underneath and result in a straighter strip. For an even neater finish, we like to use starch and press the seams open.

ADDING A SOLID BORDER/SASHING

Starch and press your top flat, then sliver trim the sides to get them straight. Measure the length of the quilt through the center to get the truest measurement. Cut the borders to the center measurement by the designated width of the strip.

Fold both the top and the border in half—creasing the centers of each—and pin together at the creases. Pin at the top and bottom as well. You can also add more folds.

If there is excess fabric, place that side against the feed dogs to help ease in the fullness. Stitch the border on without stretching.

As with strip piecing, starch the borders closed and press, then repeat once again when pressing them open.

1 Measure the length of the quilt as shown and cut side borders to match the length measurement. Sew the side borders onto the quilt top.

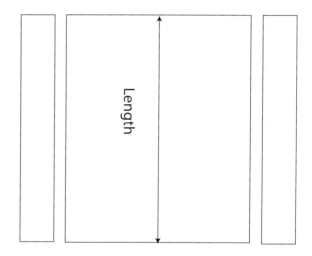

2 Once the side borders are attached, repeat the process to attach the borders on the top and bottom of the quilt.

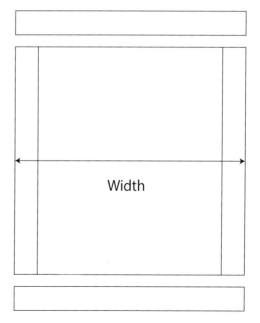

Backing Your Quilt

These days, many quilters have their own mid-arm/long-arm machine, or they "quilt by check" and send their quilts to a long-arm quilter.

Although our backing requirements take this into consideration, you should always check the requirements for a backing on every pattern that you make.

To determine the size of the backing you need, simply add 10" (25.4cm) to the finished size of the quilt top. This provides enough fabric for the long armer to load the quilt properly, and when completed, there's enough fabric for a matching hanging sleeve.

Long-arm quilters generally request that backing fabric be 4–5" (10.2–12.7cm) wider than the quilt top on each side. This will leave you with long strips, approximately 4–5" (10.2–12.7cm) wide each.

Centering the backing seam leaves the 4–5" (10.2–12.7cm) on each side. Consider using these pieces for binding.

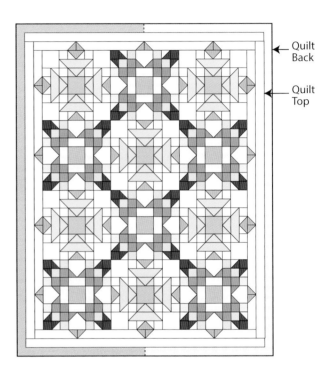

Off-centering the backing seam gives you a larger, more useable piece of fabric—with enough left over for a matching hanging sleeve.

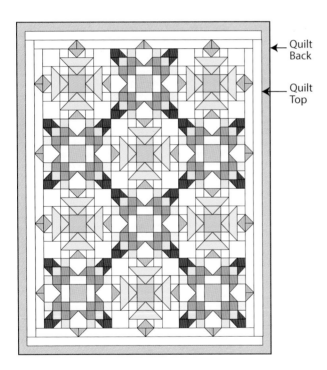

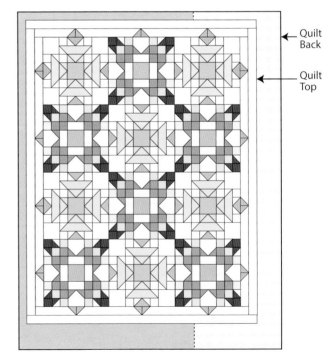

Backing fabrics let quilters have fun and use some of those interesting novelty fabrics. Backing fabrics can even become a "trademark." (Now that Linda lives in Florida, she has started using novelties with a tropical flavor.) Backings can "tell a story" about the giver or the recipient—and can even share a special "secret."

There is NO RULE that backing fabric has to match the color or "flavor" of the front fabric. Have fun!

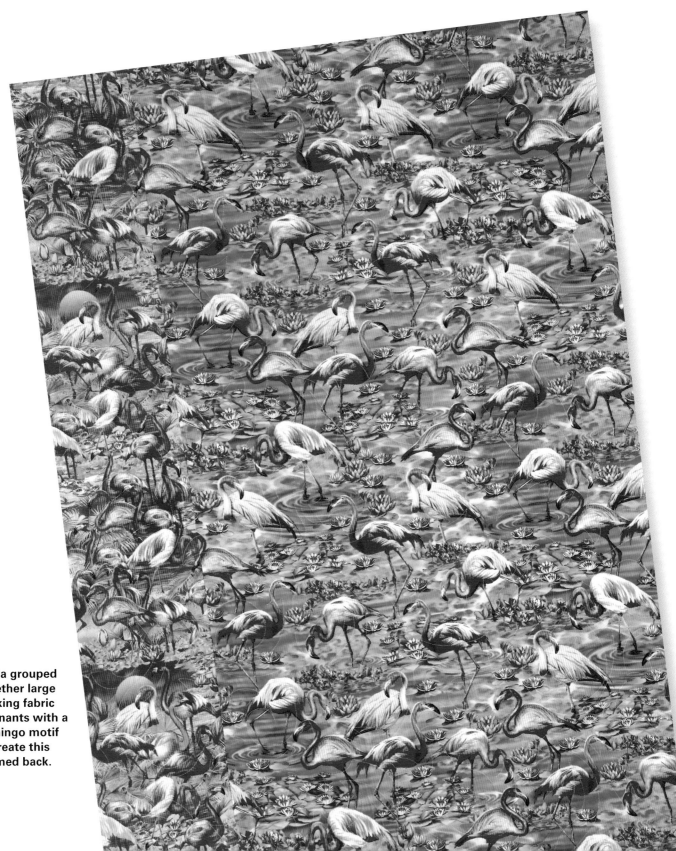

Linda grouped together large backing fabric remnants with a flamingo motif to create this themed back.

Poolside

The quilt's cool blue background reminds Linda of her favorite thing about Florida life—relaxing outside in the warm waters of her backyard pool (and no snow to shovel, ever!).

FABRIC REQUIREMENTS

* 2 yards (1.8m) Light Blue fabric
* ⅜ yard (0.3m) Medium Blue fabric
* ¾ yard (0.7m) Teal fabric
* ¾ yard (0.7m) Pink fabric
* 1⅓ yards (1.2m) Lime Green fabric
* ½ yard (0.5m) Bright Green fabric
* ½ yard (0.5m) Light Purple fabric
* 1 yard (0.9m) Dark Purple fabric
* 1¼ yards (1.1m) Bright Blue fabric
* ⅝ yard (0.6m) Binding fabric
* 4¾ yards (4.3m) Backing fabric, seamed vertically (includes enough for hanging sleeve)
* Batting for 60" x 72" (152.4cm x 182.9cm) twin size

CUTTING

From the Light Blue fabric:
(28) 5" (12.7cm) squares (HST Borders/Block 1)
(120) 2½" (6.4cm) squares (Block 2)
(20) 3" (7.6cm) squares (Block 2)
(5) 4½" (11.4cm) x WOF (width of fabric) strips (Outer Border)

From the Medium Blue fabric:
(80) 2½" (6.4cm) squares (Block 1)

From the Teal fabric:
(20) 3" (7.6cm) squares (Block 2)
(40) 2½" x 4½" (6.4cm x 11.4cm) rectangles (Block 2)

From the Pink fabric:
(40) 2½" (6.4cm) squares (Block 1)
(40) 2½" (6.4cm) squares (Block 2)
(4) 4½" (11.4cm) squares (Outer Border cornerstones)

From the Lime Green fabric:
(40) 2½" x 4½" (6.4cm x 11.4cm) rectangles (Block 2)
(28) 5" (12.7cm) squares (Block 1/Border)
(10) 4½" (11.4cm) squares (Block 1)

From the Bright Green fabric:
(80) 2½" (6.4cm) squares (Block 1)

From the Light Purple fabric:
(40) 2½" x 4½" (6.4cm x 11.4cm) rectangles (Block 2)

From the Dark Purple fabric:
(40) 2½" x 4½" (6.4cm x 11.4cm) rectangles (Block 1)
(80) 2½" (6.4cm) squares (Block 2)

From the Bright Blue fabric:
(10) 4½" (11.4cm) squares (Block 2)
(40) 2½" x 4½" (6.4cm x 11.4cm) rectangles (Block 1)
(6) 2½" (6.4cm) x WOF strips (Inner Border)

From the Binding fabric:
(7) 2½" (6.4cm) x WOF strips

From the Backing fabric:
(2) 85" (216cm) x WOF rectangles

60" x 72" (152.4cm x 182.9cm)
Made and quilted by Linda J. Hahn, Palm Bay, FL
Fabric: 1895 Collection by Hoffman California

BLOCK 1

Finished size: 12" (30.5cm) (Make 10)
Each block uses:

(2) 5" (12.7cm) squares Lime Green for HST
(1) 4½" (11.4cm) square Lime Green
(2) 5" (12.7cm) squares Light Blue for HST
(4) 2½" (6.4cm) squares Pink
(4) 2½" x 4½" (6.4cm x 11.4cm) rectangles
  Bright Blue
(8) 2½" (6.4cm) squares Bright Green
(4) 2½" x 4½" (6.4cm x 11.4cm) rectangles
  Dark Purple
(8) 2½" (6.4cm) squares Medium Blue

1 Using the 5" (12.7cm) squares of Lime Green and Light Blue, make (20) HST to yield (40). Trim to 4½" (11.4cm) square.

2 Following the Square in a Square directions on page 14, connector 2½" (6.4cm) squares of Pink onto all four corners of the 4½" (11.4cm) Lime Green square. Make (10).

3 Following the Connector Square directions on page 14, connector (2) 2½" (6.4cm) Medium Blue squares onto the 2½" x 4½" (6.4cm x 11.4cm) Dark Purple rectangles. Repeat using the 2½" (6.4cm) Bright Green squares onto the 2½" x 4½" (6.4cm x 11.4cm) Bright Blue rectangles. Make (40) of each colorway.

Stitch the Single Flying Geese units together to create a Double Flying Geese unit. Be sure to maintain the color orientation.

4 Stitch the HSTs and Double Flying Geese units together into a row. Make (20) rows.

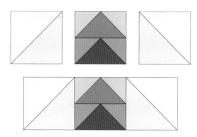

5 Stitch the remaining Double Flying Geese units to the Square-in-a-Square units. Make (10) rows.

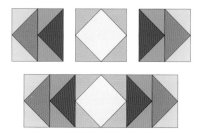

6 Stitch the rows together to complete the block. Make (10) blocks.

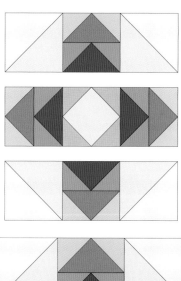

Finished Block Diagram

BLOCK 2
Finished size: 12" (30.5cm) (Make 10)
Each block uses:
(1) 4½" (11.4cm) square Bright Blue
(4) 2½" x 4½" (6.4cm x 11.4cm) rectangles
   Lime Green
(8) 2½" (6.4cm) squares Dark Purple
(4) 2½" x 4½" (6.4cm x 11.4cm) rectangles
   Light Purple
(12) 2½" (6.4cm) squares Light Blue
(2) 3" (7.6cm) squares Light Blue for HST
(2) 3" (7.6cm) squares Teal for HST
(4) 2½" x 4½" (6.4cm x 11.4cm) rectangles Teal
(4) 2½" (6.4cm) squares Pink

1 Connector 2½" (6.4cm) Light Blue squares onto the 2½" x 4½" (6.4cm x 11.4cm) Light Purple rectangle. Make (40) Single Flying Geese units.

2 Repeat using the 2½" (6.4vm) Dark Purple squares onto the 2½" x 4½" (6.4cm x 11.4cm) Lime Green rectangle. Make (40) Single Flying Geese units.

Stitch the two Single Flying Geese units together to create a Double Flying Geese unit. Be sure to maintain the color orientation. Make (40) units.

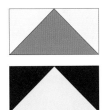 

3 Stitch a 2½" (6.4cm) Light Blue connector square onto a 2½" x 4½" (6.4cm x 11.4cm) Teal rectangle. Make (20) in each direction.

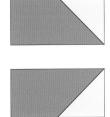

4 Following the Half-square Triangle instructions on page 11, use the 3" (7.6cm) squares of Teal and Light Blue to make (20) HST to yield a total of (40) units. Trim to 2½" (6.4cm) square.

5 Referring to the image, stitch together the units you just made as shown. Make (20) of each direction.

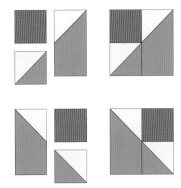

6 Stitch the Pink units and the Double Flying Geese units together into a row. Make (20) rows.

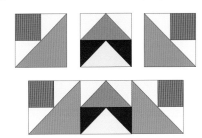

7 Stich the remaining Double Flying Geese units to the 4½" (11.4cm) Bright Blue squares. Make (10) rows.

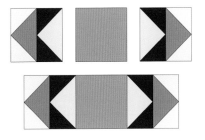

8 Stitch the rows together to complete the block. Make (10) blocks.

Finished Block Diagram

Quilt Assembly Diagram

ASSEMBLING THE QUILT TOP

Referring to the Quilt Assembly Diagram, sew the blocks together, alternating Block 1 and Block 2 to complete the quilt top.

ADD INNER BORDERS

1 Sew together the (6) 2½" (6.4cm) x WOF Bright Blue strips across the short ends to make a long border strip. From this strip, cut (2) 2½" x 60½" (6.4cm x 153.7cm) strips and (2) 2½" x 52½" (6.4cm x 133.4cm) strips.

2 Referring to the Inner Border Assembly Diagram, add the 2½" x 60½" (6.4cm x 153.7cm) Medium Blue strips to the sides.

3 Add the 2½" x 52½" (6.4cm x 133.4cm) Medium Blue strips to the top and bottom of quilt top.

Inner Border Assembly Diagram

ASSEMBLE THE PIECED OUTER BORDER

Referring to the instructions on page 11, use the 5" (12.7cm) squares of Lime Green and Light Blue to make (8) HST to yield (16) units. Trim to 4½" (11.4cm) square.

PIECE SIDE BORDERS

1 Piece together (3) 4½" (11.4cm) x WOF Light Blue strips across the short ends. Cut (2) 4½" x 48½" (11.4cm x 123.2cm) side borders.

2 Sew together (4) Lime Green/Light Blue HST units, then add a 4½" x 48½" (11.4cm x 123.2cm) Light Blue border strip to the Left side of the HST units. Make (2) side border units.

3 Referring to the Outer Border Assembly Diagram, sew the side borders in place.

TOP AND BOTTOM BORDERS

1 From the remaining 4½" (11.4cm) x WOF Light Blue strips, cut (2) 4½" x 36½" (11.4cm x 92.7cm) top/bottom borders.

2 Sew together (4) Lime Green/Light Blue HST units, then add a 4½" x 36½" (11.4cm x 92.7cm) Light Blue border strip to the Right side of the HST units.

3 Add (1) 4½" (11.4cm) Pink cornerstone to each end of the border strip. Make (2).

4 Referring to the Outer Border Assembly Diagram, sew the borders in place at the top and bottom of the quilt top.

FINISHING THE QUILT

1 Prepare the backing by stitching together the (2) 85" (216cm) x WOF cuts of backing fabric along the long edges. Layer the quilt top, batting and backing. Quilt as desired—we used an edge to edge design.

2 Use the reserved binding strips to complete the quilt. Don't forget to label your quilt!

Outer Border Assembly Diagram

Evening Breeze

Use the diagrams below to substitute fabrics from your stash to make this design your own. If you run out of one fabric, add another. The Stash version of this quilt was constructed block by block, using similar background colors and whatever colors came to hand.

BLOCK 1

For each block, you will need:

A (1) 4½" (11.4cm) square
B (4) 2½" (6.4cm) squares
C (4) 2½" x 4½" (6.4cm x 11.4cm) rectangles
D (8) 2½" (6.4cm) squares
E (4) 2½" x 4½" (6.4cm x 11.4cm) rectangles
F (8) 2½" (6.4cm) squares
G (2) 5" (12.7cm) squares for HST
H (2) 5" (12.7cm) squares for HST

BLOCK 2

For each block, you will need:

A (1) 4½" (11.4cm) square
B (4) 2½" x 4½" (6.4cm x 11.4cm) rectangles
C (8) 2½" (6.4cm) squares
D (4) 2½" x 4½" (6.4cm x 11.4cm) rectangles
E (8) 2½" (6.4cm) squares
F (4) 2½" x 4½" (6.4cm x 11.4cm) rectangles
G (4) 2½" (6.4cm) squares
H (2) 3" (7.6cm) squares for HST
I (2) 3" (7.6cm) squares for HST
J (4) 2½" (6.4cm) squares

BLOCK 1

BLOCK 2

Made and quilted by Linda J. Hahn, Palm Bay, FL
Linda made this quilt from her own stash, pulling all of the darker colors.
The toned-down palette, along with the square layout, gives it a different feel
from the bright and lively original. No two blocks are the same!

Cash

Starshine

The use of black and white along with Linda's preferred bright colors makes this a striking quilt with crisp, modern lines.

FABRIC REQUIREMENTS

* ½ yard (0.5m) Green fabric
* ¾ yard (0.7m) Blue fabric
* ¼ yard (0.2m) Orange fabric
* ⅓ yard (0.3m) Purple fabric
* ⅓ yard (0.3m) Pink fabric
* 3¼ yards (3m) White fabric
* 2 yards (1.8m) Black fabric
* ½ yard (0.5m) Binding fabric
* 4 yards (3.7m) Backing fabric
* Batting for 56" (142cm) square quilt top

CUTTING

From the Green fabric:
(56) 2½" (6.4cm) squares
(8) 3" (7.6cm) squares

From the Blue fabric:
(16) 2½" (6.4cm) squares
(18) 3" (7.6cm) squares
(40) 2½" x 4½" (6.4cm x 11.4cm) rectangles

From the Orange fabric:
(20) 2½" (6.4cm) squares

From the Purple fabric:
(20) 2½" (6.5cm) squares
(10) 3" (7.6cm) squares

From the Pink fabric:
(20) 2½" (7.6cm) squares
(10) 3" (7.6cm) squares

From the White fabric:
(36) 4½" (11.4cm) squares (Blocks)
(100) 2½" (6.4cm) squares (Block 1)
(96) 2½" (6.4cm) squares (Block 2)
(20) 3" (7.6cm) squares (Block 1)
(8) 3" (7.6cm) squares (Block 2)
(4) 4½" (11.4cm) squares (Border Corner)
(12) 4½" x 16½" (11.4cm x 41.9cm) rectangles (Border)

From the Black fabric:
(40) 2½" x 4½" (6.4cm x 11.4cm) rectangles (Block 1)
(48) 2½" x 4½" (6.4cm x 11.4cm) rectangles (Block 2)
(40) 2½" (6.4cm) squares (Block 1)
(48) 2½" (6.4cm) squares (Block 2)
(10) 3" (7.6cm) squares (Block 1)
(8) 3" (7.6cm) squares (Block 2)
(16) 4½" 11.4cm) squares (Border)

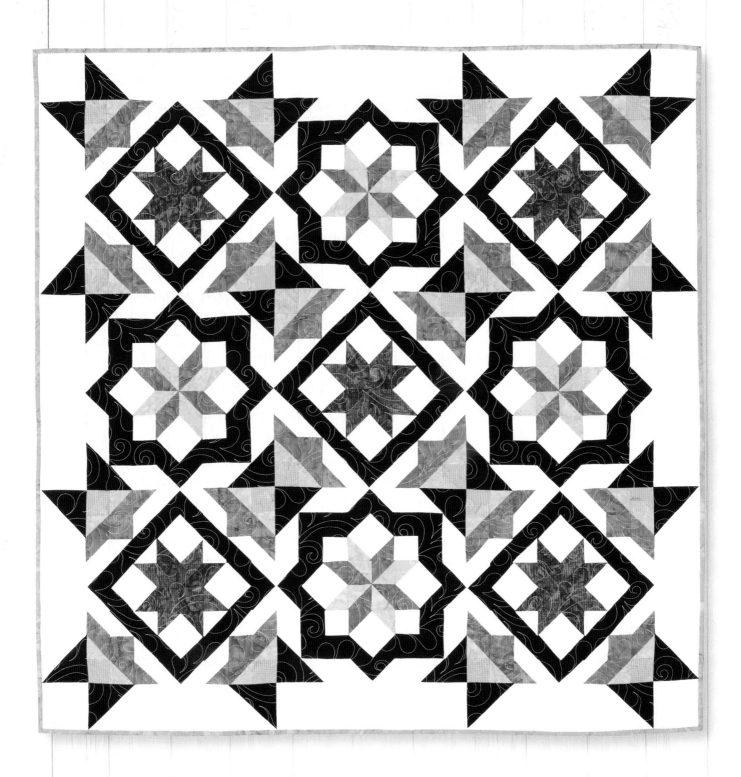

56" (142.2cm) Square
Made and quilted by Linda J. Hahn, Palm Bay, FL
Fabric: 1895 Collection by Hoffman California

BLOCK 1
Finished Size: 16" (40.6cm) (Make 5)
Each block uses:
(4) 2½" (6.4cm) squares Orange
(2) 3" (7.6cm) squares each of Purple and Pink
(2) 3" (7.6cm) squares of Blue
(8) 2½" x 4½" (6.4cm x 11.4cm) rectangles Blue
(20) 2½" (6.4cm) squares White
(8) 2½" x 4½" (6.4cm x 11.4cm) rectangles Black
(4) 2½" (6.4cm) squares each of Purple and Pink
(8) 2½" (6.4cm) squares Black
(4) 4½" (11.4cm) squares White
(8) 2½" (6.4cm) squares Green
(4) 3" (7.6cm) squares White
(2) 3" (7.6cm) squares Black

1 Use (2) 3" (7.6cm) squares each of Purple and Pink to make (4) HST units. Trim to 2½" (6.4cm) square. Referring to the image for color orientation, stitch the HST together to form a Pinwheel.

2 Use (2) 3" (7.6cm) squares each of White and Black to make (4) HST units. Trim to 2½" (7.6cm) square. Then use (2) 3" (7.6cm) squares each of White and Blue to make (4) HST units. Trim to 2½" (7.6cm) square.

3 Noting the orientation of the connector square, connector a 2½" (6.4cm) White square onto either side of a 2½" x 4½" (6.4cm x 11.4cm) Black rectangle. Make (4) units.

4 Noting the orientation of the connector square, connector a 2½" (6.4cm) Green square onto the left side of a 2½" x 4½" (6.4cm x 11.4cm) Blue rectangle and a 2½" (7.6cm) White square onto the right side. Make (4) units.

5 Noting the orientation of the connector square, connector a 2½" (7.6cm) Green square onto the left side of a 2½" x 4½" (6.4cm x 11.4cm) Blue rectangle. Make (4) units.

6 Connector a 2½" (6.4cm) White square onto each side of a 2½" x 4½" (6.4cm x 11.4cm) Black rectangle. Make (4) units.

7 Noting the orientation of the connector square, connector a 2½" (6.4cm) Black square onto the Top left and right corners of a 4½" (11.4cm) White square. Connector a 2½" (6.4cm) Purple square on the Bottom left and a 2½" (6.4cm) Pink square onto the Bottom right. Make (4) SIS (Square in a Square) units.

8 Stitch the Black/White Flying Geese unit onto the top of the SIS unit. Make (4) units.

9 Referring to the image, stitch together the remaining units, adding a 2½" (6.4cm) Orange square. Make (4) corner units.

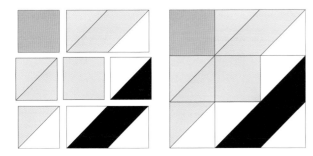

10 Stitch the units together into rows, then stitch the rows together to form the block. Make (5) blocks.

Finished Block Diagram

BLOCK 2
Finished size 16" (40.6cm)   (Make 4)
Each block uses:
(2) 3" (7.6cm) squares each of Green, Blue, White, and Black
(4) 2½" (6.4cm) squares each of Green and Blue
(4) 4½" (11.4cm) White squares
(12) 2½" x 4½" (6.4cm x 11.4cm) Black rectangles
(24) 2½" (6.4cm) White squares
(12) 2½" (6.4cm) Black squares

1 Use (2) 3" squares each of Green and Blue to make (4) HST. Trim to 2½" (6.4cm) square. Stitch together to form a pinwheel, paying close attention to the color placement. Make (1) unit.

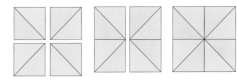

2 Use (2) 3" (7.6cm) squares each of Black and White to make (4) HST units. Trim to 2½" (6.4cm) square.

3 Noting the orientation of the connector square, connector a 2½" (6.4cm) Black square onto the Top left and right corners of a 4½" (11.4cm) White square. Connector a 2½" (6.4cm) Green square on the Bottom left and a 2½" (6.4cm) Blue square onto the Bottom right. Make (4) SIS units.

4 Connector a 2½" (6.4cm) White square onto each side of a 2½" x 4½" (6.4cm x 11.4cm) Black rectangle. Make (4) units.

5 Connector a 2½" (6.4cm) White square onto one side of a 2½" x 4½" (6.4cm x 11.4cm) Black rectangle. Make (4) units.

6 Referring to the diagram, stitch a 2½" (6.4cm) White square onto the Black/White rectangle. Make (4) units.

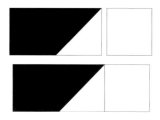

7 Stitch the Black/White HST to a 2½" x 4½" (6.4cm x 11.4cm) Black rectangle. Make (4) units.

8 Stitch a 2½" (6.4cm) White Square to each side of a 2½" (6.4cm) Black square. Make (4) units.

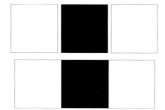

9 Referring to the diagram, assemble the Black and White units into a Nine Patch. Make (4) units.

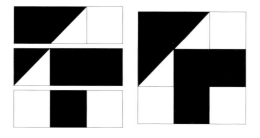

10 Stitch the Black/White Flying Geese unit to the top of the SIS unit. Make (4) units.

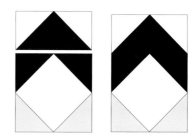

11 Referring to the image, stitch the units into rows and the rows into the block. Make (4) blocks.

Finished Block Diagram

COMPLETE THE QUILT TOP

1 Sew the blocks together into rows of three, alternating Block 1 and Block 2.

2 Sew the rows together to complete the quilt top.

Quilt Assembly Diagram

CONSTRUCT PIECED BORDER

1 Connector a 4½" (11.4cm) Black square onto each end of a 4½" x 16½" (11.6cm x 42cm) White rectangle, noting the placement of the connector squares. Make (8) units.

2 Sew one of the Black/White units to either side of a 4½" x 16½" (11.4cm x 42cm) White rectangle. Make (4) units.

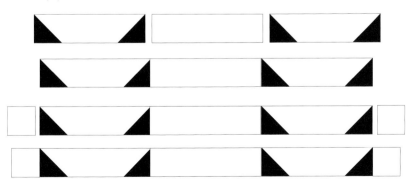

3 Sew two pieced borders to either side of the quilt top with the points oriented out. Add a 4½" (11.4cm) White square to either side of the remaining border units. Sew the units to the top and bottom of the quilt top.

Border Assembly Diagram

FINISHING THE QUILT

1 Press the quilt top. Layer and baste. Quilt as desired!

2 Bind the quilt using 2½" (6.4cm) x WOF strips. Don't forget the label!

Moonshine

Color the quilt your way! Refer to the diagram for the cut sizes of the patches needed for each block. Make copies of the block diagram if needed to help determine where to put each color.

BLOCK 1

For each block, you will need:

A/B (2) 3" (7.6cm) squares of each color for HST
C/D (4) 2½" (6.4cm) squares of each color for connectors
E (4) 4½" (11.4cm) squares for SIS
F (8) 2½" (6.4cm) squares for connectors
G (4) 2½" x 4½" (6.4cm x 11.4cm) rectangles
H (8) 2½" (6.4cm) squares for connectors
I (8) 2½" (6.4cm) squares for connectors
J (4) 2½" x 4½" (6.4cm x 11.4cm) rectangles
K/L (2) 3" (7.6cm) squares of each color for HST
M (4) 2½" x 4½" (6.4cm x 11.4cm) rectangles
N/O (2) 3" (7.6cm) squares of each color for HST
P (4) 2½" (6.4cm) squares for connectors
Q (4) 2½" (6.4cm) squares
R (4) 2½" x 4½" (6.4cm x 11.4cm) rectangles
S/T (4) 2½" (6.4cm) squares of each color for connectors

BLOCK 2

For each block, you will need:

A/B (2) 3" (7.6cm) squares of each color for HST
C/D (4) 2½" (6.4cm) squares of each color for connectors
E (4) 4½" (11.4cm) squares for SIS
F (8) 2½" (6.4cm) squares for connectors
G (4) 2½" x 4½" (6.4cm x 11.4cm) rectangles
H (8) 2½" (6.4cm) squares for connectors
I (8) 2½" (6.4cm) squares
J (4) 2½" (6.4cm) squares
K/L (2) 3" (7.6cm) squares of each color for HST
M (4) 2½" x 4½" (6.4cm x 11.4cm) rectangles
N (4) 2½" x 4½" (6.4cm x 11.4cm) rectangles
O (4) 2½" (6.4cm) squares for connectors
P (4) 2½" (6.4cm) squares

BLOCK 1

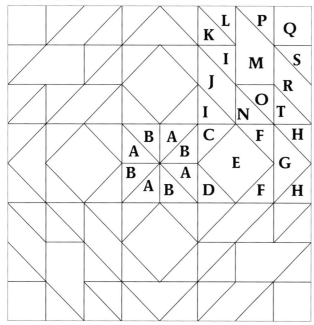

BLOCK 2

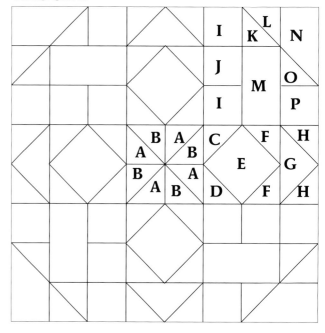

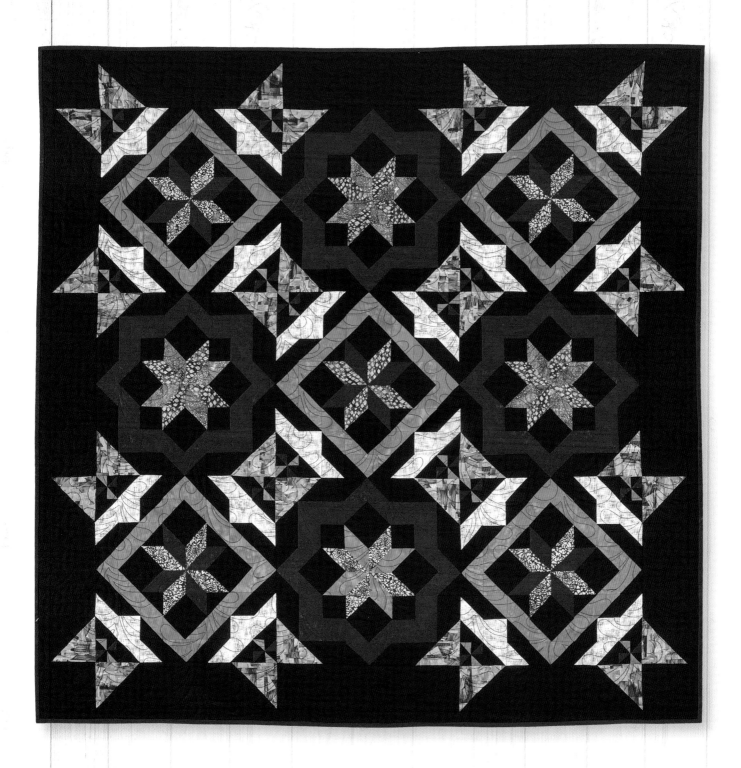

Made by Linda J. Hallatt, Canton, NC
Quilted by Linda J. Hahn
Linda Hallatt's version of this Starshine quilt features multicolored prints on a
black background with the substitution of mini (2" [5.1cm] finished!) pinwheels
in the corners of Block 1 and an added 1" (2.5cm) solid border.

Rose Garden

Linda's clever placement of colors turns blocks into flowers
and leaves in this cheerful, lively quilt.

FABRIC REQUIREMENTS

* 3 yards (2.7m) White fabric
* 1¼ yards (1.1m) Lime Green fabric
* ½ yard (0.5m) Orange fabric
* ⅓ yard (0.3m) Blue fabric
* ¼ yard (0.2m) Teal fabric
* ½ yard (0.5m) Dark Pink fabric
* ⅔ yard (0.6m) Orange-Red fabric
* ⅓ yard (0.3m) Gold fabric
* ¼ yard (0.2m) Pink fabric
* ⅝ yard (0.6m) Binding fabric
* 4¾ yards (4.3m) Backing fabric, seamed vertically
* Batting for 57"x 73" (145cm x 185.4cm) quilt top (twin size)

CUTTING

From the White fabric:
(24) 4½" (11.4cm) squares (Block 2)
(24) 4½" (11.4cm) squares (Block 1)
(24) 2½" (6.4cm) squares (Block 2)
(168) 2½" (6.4) squares (Block 1)
(12) 3" (7.6cm) squares (Block 2)
(4) 2½" x 8½" (6.4cm x 21.6cm) rectangles (Border)
(4) 2½" x 10½" (6.4cm x 26.7cm) rectangles (Border)
(10) 2½" x 16½" (6.4cm x 41.9cm) rectangles (Border)
(7) 2½" (6.4cm) x Width of fabric (WOF) strips (Second Border)

From the Lime Green fabric:
(24) 2½" x 4½" rectangles (6.4cm x 11.4cm) (Block 1)
(24) 2½" x 8½" (6.4cm x 21.6cm) rectangles (Block 1)
(72) 2½" (6.4cm) squares (Block 2)

From the Orange fabric:
(24) 2½" x 4½" (6.4cm x 11.4cm) rectangles (Block 1)
(28) 2½" (6.4cm) squares (Border)

From the Blue fabric:
(48) 2½" (6.4cm) squares (Block 1)

From the Teal fabric:
(6) 4½" (11.4cm) squares (Block 1)

From the Dark Pink fabric:
(24) 2½" x 4½" (6.4cm x 11.4cm) rectangles (Block 2)
(12) 3" (7.6cm) squares (Block 2)

From the Orange-Red fabric:
(120) 2½" (6.4cm) squares (Block 2)

From the Gold fabric:
(24) 2½" x 4½" (6.4cm x 11.4cm) rectangles (Block 2)

From the Pink fabric:
(6) 4½" (11.4cm) squares (Block 2)

From the Binding fabric:
(7) 2½" (6.4cm) x WOF strips

Finished Size: 57" x 73" (135cm x 185.4cm)
Made and quilted by Linda J. Hahn, Palm Bay, FL
Fabric: 1895 Collection from Hoffman California

BLOCK 1

Finished size: 16" (40.6cm) (Make 6)
Each Block Uses:

(4) 4½" (11.4cm) squares White
(28) 2½" (6.4cm) squares White
(4) 2½" X 4½" (6.4cm x 11.4cm) rectangles
    Lime Green
(4) 2½" x 8½" (6.4cm x 21.6cm) rectangles
    Lime Green
 (4) 2½" X 4½" (6.4cm x 11.4cm)
    rectangles Orange
(1) 4½" (11.4cm) square Teal
(8) 2½" (6.4cm) squares Blue

1 Using the 2½" x 4½" (6.4cm x 11.4cm) rectangles as the base and 2½" (6.4cm) squares for connectors, make (4) single Flying Geese of each combination:

2 Add a 2½" (6.4cm) White square to the ends of two of the Blue/Lime Green Flying geese units. Add a 2½" (6.4cm) White square to each end of all of the White/Orange Flying Geese units.

 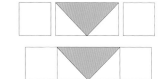

3 Connector a 2½" (6.4cm) White square onto the ends of a 2½" x 8½" (6.4cm x 21.6cm) Lime Green rectangle. Make (4) units.

4 Stitch all of the Orange/White units to the Lime Green/White units, paying attention to the orientation of the pieces. Make (4) units.

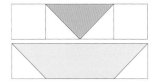 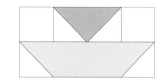

5 Stitch a 4½" (11.6cm) White square to either side of two of the units from step 4.

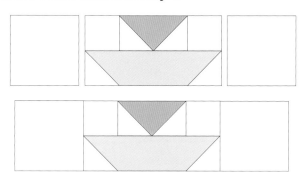

6 Stitch the two remaining Blue/Green Flying Geese units to the sides of a 4½" (11.6cm) Teal square.

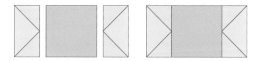

7 Attach the Blue/Lime Green/White units to the top and bottom of the Teal Square unit.

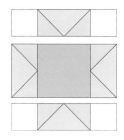 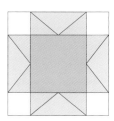

8 Stitch the Orange/Lime Green/White units to the sides of the Teal/Blue/Green star unit.

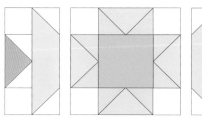

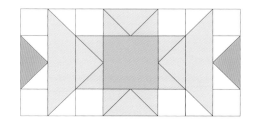

9 Finally, attach the remaining units to the top and bottom of the block. Give it a good press. Make (6) blocks.

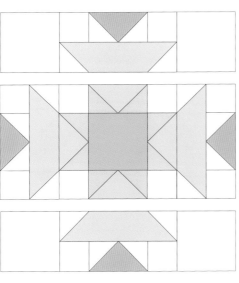

Finished Block Diagram

BLOCK 2
Finished Size: 16" (40.6cm) (Make 6)
Each block uses:
(4) 4½" (11.4cm) squares White
(2) 3" (7.6cm) squares White for HST
(4) 2½" (6.4cm) squares White
(4) 2½" x 4½" (6.4cm x 11.4cm) rectangles Gold
(1) 4½" (11.4cm) square Pink
(12) 2½" (6.4cm) squares Lime Green
(20) 2½" (6.4cm) squares Orange-Red
(4) 2½" x 4½" (6.4cm x 11.4cm) rectangles
    Dark Pink
(2) 3" (7.6cm) squares Dark Pink for HST

1 Stitch together a 2½" (6.4cm) Lime Green square and a 2½" (6.4cm) Orange-Red square. Make (8) units.

2 Connector a 2½" (6.4cm) Orange-Red square onto two corners of a 4½" (11.4cm) White squares. Make (4) units.

3 Stitch an Orange-Red/Lime Green unit to either side of an Orange-Red/White unit. Make (4) units.

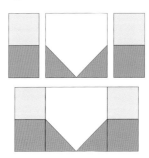

4 Connector a 2½" (6.4cm) White square onto a 2½" x 4½" (6.4cm x 11.4cm) Dark Pink rectangle, noting the orientation of the connector square. Make (4) units.

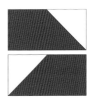

5 Use the 3" (7.6cm) squares of White and Dark Pink to make a total of (4) HST units. Trim to 2½" (6.4cm) square.

6 Referring to the images, stich together a Dark Pink/White rectangle unit, a Red/White HST and a 2½" (6m4cm) square each of Lime Green and Orange-Red. Make two side units in each direction.

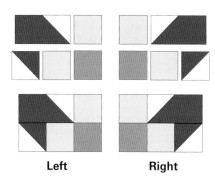

Left   Right

7 Stich a 2½" x 4½" (6.4cm x 11.4cm) Gold rectangle onto each side of the 4½" (11.4cm) Pink square.

8 Then stitch a 2½" (6.4cm) Orange-Red square onto each side of the remaining Gold rectangles.

9 Stitch the Orange-Red/Gold rectangle unit to the top and bottom of the Gold/Pink unit.

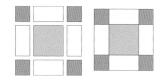

Refer to this image for steps 7–9

10 Attach an Orange-Red/Lime Green/White unit to each side of the block you just made.

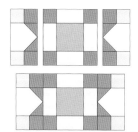

11 Paying careful attention to the orientation of the side units, stitch a side unit to the White/Orange-Red unit. Make 2 units.

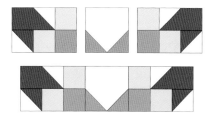

12 Stitch the rows together to form the block. Make (6) blocks.

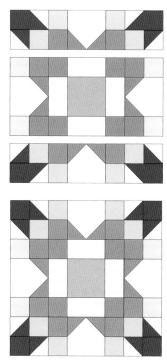

Finished Block Diagram

COMPLETE QUILT TOP

1 Sew the blocks together, alternating Block 1 and Block 2. Stich the rows together to complete the quilt top.

Quilt Assembly Diagram

CONSTRUCT THE PIECED BORDER

1 Connector a 2½" (6.4cm) Orange square onto each end of a 2½" x 16½" (6.4cm x 41.9cm) rectangle, noting the placement of the connector squares. Make (10) units.

2 Connector a 2½" (6.4cm) Orange square onto one end of a 2½" x 8½" (6.4cm x 21.6cm) rectangle, noting the placement of the connector squares. Make (2) units of each configuration.

3 Sew together (3) of the 16 ½" (41.9cm) units you just made, adding an 8 ½" (21.6cm) unit on each end. Make (2) side borders. Sew a pieced side border to each side of the finished quilt top, orienting the points out.

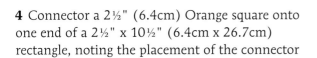

4 Connector a 2½" (6.4cm) Orange square onto one end of a 2½" x 10½" (6.4cm x 26.7cm) rectangle, noting the placement of the connector squares. Make (2) units of each configuration.

5 Repeating the steps above, sew together (2) of the 16½" (41.9cm) units you just made. Sew a 10½" (26.7cm) unit on each end. Make (2) borders.

6 Sew a pieced border to the top and bottom of the finished quilt top, orienting the points out.

Pieced Border Diagram

ADDING SECOND BORDER

1 Sew the White 2½" (6.4cm) x WOF strips together into one long strip. From the strip, cut (2) 2½" x 68½" (6.4cm x 174cm) side borders. Sew a side border to either side of the quilt top.

2 Cut (2) 2½" x 56½" (6.4cm x 144cm) strips. Sew the strips to the top and bottom of the quilt top.

FINISHING THE QUILT

1 Give the quilt top a good press. Layer and baste. Quilt as desired—we used an edge-to-edge design.

2 Bind the quilt using 2½" (6.4cm) x WOF strips. Don't forget the label!

Second Border Quilt Diagram

Orange Crush

Use up your scraps and make every block different! If you
run out of a fabric, use another of the same value.

BLOCK 1

For each block, you will need:

- **A** (1) 4½" (11.4cm) square
- **B** (4) 2½" x 4½" (6.4cm x 11.4cm) rectangle
- **C** (8) 2½" (6.4cm) squares for connectors
- **D** (4) 2½" (6.4cm) squares
- **E** (8) 2½" (6.4cm) squares for connectors
- **F** (4) 2½" x 8½" (6.4cm x 21.6cm) rectangles
- **G** (8) 2½" (21.6cm) squares for connectors
- **H** (4) 2½" x 4½" (6.4cm x 11.4cm) rectangles
- **I** (8) 2½" (6.4cm) squares
- **J** (4) 4½" (11.4cm) squares

BLOCK 2

For each block, you will need:

- **A** (1) 4½" (11.4cm) square
- **B** (4) 2½" x 4½" (6.4cm x 11.4cm) rectangle
- **C** (8) 2½" (6.4cm) squares for connectors
- **D** (4) 4½" (11.4cm) squares
- **E** (12) 2½" (6.4cm) squares
- **F** (12) 2½" (6.4cm) squares
- **G/H** (2) 3" (7.6cm) squares of each color for HST
- **I** (4) 2½" x 4½" (6.4cm x 11.4cm) rectangles
- **J** (4) 2½" (6.4cm) squares for connectors

BLOCK 1

BLOCK 2

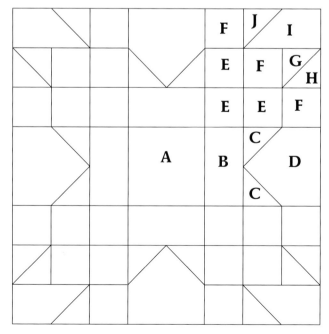

Made by Carmen Solomon, Seymour, TN
Quilted by Linda J. Hahn, Palm Bay, FL
Carmen Solomon's version of this quilt uses a wide variety of batik scraps, making
each block different, all centered on an eye-catching orange background. She also
added more borders, alternating solid borders and thin scrappy pieced lines.

Sparkler

Linda's choice of bright batiks makes these quilt blocks "explode" into shards of light.

FABRIC REQUIREMENTS

* 2½ yards (2.3m) White fabric
* ½ yard (0.5cm) Lime Green fabric
* ⅓ yard (0.3m) Orange fabric
* ½ yard (0.5m) Blue fabric
* ⅔ yard (0.6m) Purple fabric
* ½ yard (0.5m) Teal fabric
* ⅓ yard (0.3m) Yellow fabric
* 1 yard (0.9m) Hot Pink fabric
* ⅛ yard (0.1m) Pink fabric
* ⅛ yard (0.1m) Dark Pink fabric
* ⅓ yard (0.3m) Red-Orange fabric
* ⅝ yard (0.6m) Binding fabric
* 4¾ yards (4.3m) Backing fabric (seamed vertically)
* Batting for 53"x 68" (134.6cm x 172.7cm) quilt top (twin size)

CUTTING

From the White fabric:
(144) 2½" (6.4cm) squares (Block 1)
(48) 2½" x 6½" (6.4cm x 16.5cm) rectangles (Block 1)
(144) 2½" (6.4cm) squares (Block 2)
(6) 4½" (11.4cm) squares (Block 2)
(14) 2½" x 12½" (6.4cm x 31.8cm) rectangles (Border)

From the Lime Green fabric:
(36) 2½" (6.4cm) squares (Block 1)
(24) 2½" (6.4cm) squares (Block 2)
(16) 2½" (6.4cm) squares (Border)

From the Orange fabric:
(48) 2½" (6.4cm) squares (Block 1)

From the Blue fabric:
(12) 2½" (6.4cm) squares (Block 1)
(24) 2½" (6.4cm) squares (Block 2)
(16) 2½" (6.4cm) squares (Border)

From the Purple fabric:
(24) 2½" (6.4cm) squares (Block 1)
(48) 2½" x 4½" (6.4cm x 11.4cm) rectangles (Block 2)

From the Teal fabric:
(24) 2½" x 4½" (6.4cm x 11.4cm) rectangles (Block 1)
(24) 2½" x 4½" (6.4cm x 11.4cm) rectangles (Block 2)

From the Yellow fabric:
(48) 2½" (6.4cm) squares (Block 2)

From the Hot Pink fabric:
(48) 2½" x 4½" (6.4cm x 11.4cm) rectangles (Block 2)
(72) 2½" (6.4cm) squares (Block 2)

From the Pink fabric:
(12) 2½" (6.4cm) squares (Block 1)

From the Dark Pink fabric:
(12) 2½" (6.4cm) squares (Block 1)

From the Red-Orange fabric:
(24) 2½" x 4½" (6.4cm x 11.4cm) rectangles (Block 1)

53" x 68" (134.6cm x 172.7cm)
Made and quilted by Linda J. Hahn, Palm Bay, FL
Fabric Collection: 1895 Collection by Hoffman California

BLOCK 1
Finished Size: 16" (40.6cm) (Make 6)
Each block uses:
(24) 2½" (6.4cm) squares (Connectors) White
(8) 2½" x 6½" (6.4cm x16.5cm) rectangles White
(4) 2½" x 4½" (6.4cm x 11.4cm) rectangles Teal
(2) 2½" (6.4cm) squares Dark Pink
(2) 2½" (6.4cm) squares Pink
(4) 2½" x 4½" (6.4cm x 11.4cm) rectangles
  Red-Orange
(8) 2½" (6.4cm) squares (Connectors) Orange
(4) 2½" (6.4cm) squares Purple
(6) 2½" (6.4cm) squares Lime Green
(2) 2½" (6.4cm) squares Blue

1 Using 2½" (6.4cm) squares of Purple, Dark Pink, and White, make (2) Four Patch units. Make (2) units using 2½" (6.4cm) squares Purple, Pink, and White. Make (1) unit using 2½" (6.4cm) squares of Blue and Lime Green.

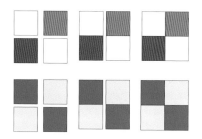

2 Using 2½" x 4½" (6.4cm x 11.4cm) rectangles of Red-Orange and Teal with 2½" (6.4cm) square White connectors, make (4) Flying Geese units of each combination. Referring to the diagram, sew 2 units together. Make (4) units.

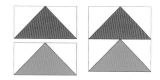

3 Stich together (1) 2½" x 6½" (6.4cm x 16.5cm) White rectangle and (1) 2½" (6.4cm) square Orange connector. Referring to the diagram, make (4) units of each orientation. Stitch together 2 of the Orange/White units. Make (4) units.

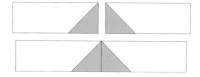

4 Add a 2½" (6.4cm) Lime Green square to the sides of two of the Orange/White units.

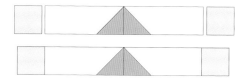

5 Sew the units together into rows, noting the orientation of the units. Stitch the rows together.

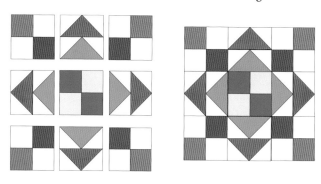

6 Sew a White/Orange unit onto each side of the block. Sew a White/Orange/Lime Green unit onto the top and bottom of the block. Make 6 blocks.

Finished Block Diagram

BLOCK 2
Finished Size: 16" (Make 6)
Each block uses:
(24) 2½" (6.4cm) squares White
(1) 4½" (11.4cm) square White
(4) 2½" x 4½" (6.4cm x 11.4cm) rectangles Teal
(4) 2½" (6.4cm) squares Lime Green
(8) 2½" (6.4cm) squares Yellow (Connectors)
(8) 2½" x 4½" (6.4cm x 11.4cm) rectangles Purple
(8) 2½" (6.4cm) squares Hot Pink (Connectors)
(4) 2½" (6.4cm) squares Hot Pink
(8) 2½" x 4½" (6.4cm x 11.4cm) rectangles
    Hot Pink
(4) 2½" (6.4cm) squares Blue

1 Using 2½" (6.4cm) squares of White, Blue, and
Hot Pink, make (4) Four Patch units.

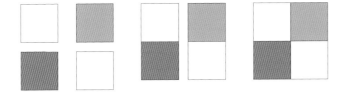

2. Sew together (4) 2½" (6.4cm) squares of Lime
Green, (4) 2½" x 4½" (6.4cm x 11.4cm) rectangles
of Teal, and (1) 4½" square of White. Make
(1) unit.

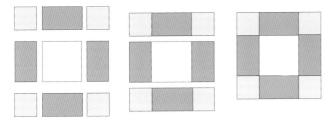

3 Connector a 2½" (6.4cm) Hot Pink square
and a 2½" (6.4cm) White square to a 2½" x 4½"
(6.4cm x 11.4cm) Purple rectangle, noting the
orientation of the connectors. Make (4) units in
each orientation. Connector a 2½" (6.4cm) Yellow
square and a 2½" (6.4cm) White square to a 2½" x
4½" (6.4cm x 11.4cm) Hot Pink rectangle, noting
the orientation of the connectors. Make (4) units in
each orientation.

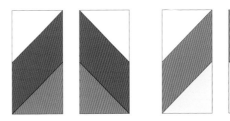

4 Sew (2) Yellow/Hot Pink/White units together.
Make (4) units. Sew a Hot Pink/Purple/White unit
on either side of the Yellow/Hot Pink/White units
as shown.

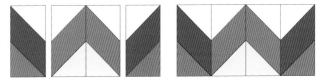

5 Referring to the diagram, sew the units together
into rows.

6 Referring to the diagram, sew the rows together to complete block. Repeat the steps to make a total of (6) blocks.

Finished Block Diagram

COMPLETE QUILT TOP

1 Referring to the diagram, sew the blocks together into rows, alternating Block 1 and Block 2.

Quilt Assembly Diagram

PIECING THE BORDERS

1 Add 2½" (6.4cm) Blue squares to each end of a 2½" x 12½" (6.4cm x 31.8cm) White rectangle. Make (7) units. Add 2½" (6.4cm) Lime Green squares to each end of a 2½" x 12½" (6.4cm x 31.8cm) White rectangle. Make (7) units.

SIDE BORDERS

1 Sew together (2) Blue/White units and (2) Lime Green/White units to form the side border. Make (2) units with the same configuration.

2 Sew a border in place along each side of the quilt top, noting the orientation of the border with the Blue end at the bottom to maintain the Four Patch corners.

TOP BORDER

1 Sew together (2) Lime Green/White units and (1) Blue/White unit to form the top border. Add a 2½" (6.4cm) Blue square to each end of the border units.

2 Sew the border in place along the top edge of the quilt top.

BOTTOM BORDER

1 Sew together (2) Blue/White units and (1) Lime Green/White unit to form the bottom border. Add a 2½" (6.4cm) Lime Green square to each end of the border. Sew in place along the bottom edge of quilt top.

FINISHING THE QUILT

1 Give the quilt top a good press. Layer and baste. Quilt as desired!

2 Bind the quilt using 2½" (6.4cm) x WOF strips. Don't forget the label!

Pieced Border Diagram

Sunrise

Color the quilt YOUR way! Refer to the diagram for the cut sizes of the patches needed for each block. If needed, make copies of the black-and-white block to help determine where to place each color.

BLOCK 1
For each block, you will need:
- **A** (2) 2½" (6.4cm) squares
- **B** (2) 2½" (6.4cm) squares
- **C** (4) 2½" x 4½" (6.4c x 11.4cm) rectangles
- **D** (8) 2½" (6.4cm) squares for connectors
- **E** (4) 2½" x 4½" (6.4cm x 11.4cm) rectangles
- **F** (8) 2½" (6.4cm) squares for connectors
- **G** (8) 2½" (6.4cm) squares
- **H** (8) 2½" (6.4cm) squares
- **I** (8) 2½" x 6½" (6.4cm x 15.5cm) rectangles
- **J** (8) 2½" (6.4cm) squares for connectors
- **K** (4) 2½" (6.4cm) squares

BLOCK 2
For each block, you will need:
- **A** (1) 4½" (6.4cm) square
- **B** (4) 2½" x 4½" (6.4cm x 11.4cm) rectangles
- **C** (4) 2½" (6.4cm) squares
- **D** (8) 2½" x 4½" (6.4cm x 11.4cm) rectangles
- **E** (8) 2½" (6.4cm) squares for connectors
- **F** (8) 2½" (6.4cm) squares for connectors
- **G** (8) 2½" x 4½" (6.4cm x 11.4cm) rectangles
- **H** (8) 2½" (6.4cm) squares for connectors
- **I** (8) 2½" (6.4cm) squares for connectors
- **J** (4) 2½" (6.4cm) squares
- **K** (8) 2½" (6.4cm) squares
- **L** (4) 2½" (6.4cm) squares

BLOCK 1

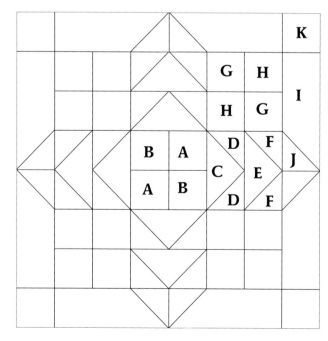

BLOCK 2

Made by Amy D. Chaney, Maryville, TN
Quilted by Linda J. Hahn, Palm Bay, FL
Amy Chaney used bright batiks from her stash with a healthy dose of
yellow and reds. A cool blue background rounds out the palette.

Summer Splash

The warm colors of this quilt remind Anne-Marie of summers at the Jersey Shore.

FABRIC REQUIREMENTS

* 3 yards (2.7m) White fabric
* 1 yard (0.9m) Pink fabric (Linda used several different shades)
* 1¼ yards (1.1m) Lime Green fabric
* 1¼ yards (1.1m) Orange fabric
* ½ yard (0.5m) Dark Pink fabric
* ½ yard (0.5) Gold fabric
* ⅔ yard (0.6m) Binding fabric
* 4-¾ yards (4.3m) Backing fabric (seamed vertically)
* Batting for a 67" x 77" (170.1cm x 195.6cm) quilt top (twin size)

CUTTING

From the White fabric:
(60) 3" (7.6cm) squares (Block 1)
(60) 2½" (6.4cm) squares (Block 1)
(120) 1½ (3.8cm) squares (Block 2)
(180) 2½" (6.4cm) squares (Block 2)
(15) 2½" (6.4cm) x width of border (WOF) strips (Borders)

From the Pink fabric:
(30) 3" (7.6cm) squares (Block 1)
(60) 2½" x 4½" (6.4cm x 11.4cm) rectangles (Block 1)

From the Lime Green fabric:
(60) 2½" (6.4cm) squares (Block 1)
(30) 3" (7.6cm) squares for HST (Block 1)
(6) 2½" (6.4cm) x WOF strip (First Border)

From the Orange fabric:
(60) 2½" (6.4cm) squares (Block 1)
(75) 2½" (6.4cm) squares (Block 2)
(60) 1½" (3.8cm) squares (Block 2)
(3) 2½" (6.4cm) x WOF strips (Pieced Border)

From the Dark Pink fabric:
(15) 2½" (6.4cm) squares (Block 1)
(60) 1½" (3.8cm) squares (Block 2)
(3) 2½" (6.4cm) x WOF strips (Pieced Border)

From the Gold fabric:
(60) 2½" (6.4cm) squares (Block 2)
(3) 2½" (6.4cm) x WOF strips (Pieced Border)

From the Binding fabric:
(8) 2½" (6.4cm) x WOF strips

67" x 77" (170.1cm x 195.6cm)
Made by Anne-Marie Neumann, Freehold, NJ. Quilted by Deborah G. Stanley, Matawan, NJ
Fabric: Canvas, Dublin and Toscana Collections from Banyan
Batiks by Northcott Silk

BLOCK 1
Finished Size: 10" (25.4cm) (Make 5)
Each block uses:
(4) 3" (7.6cm) squares White for HST
(4) 2½" (6.4cm) squares White
(2) 3" (7.6cm) squares Pink for HST
(4) 2½" x 4½" (6.4cm x 11.4cm) rectangles Pink
(2) 3" (7.6cm) squares Lime Green for HST
(4) 2½" (6.4cm) squares Lime Green
(4) 2½" (6.4cm) squares Orange
(1) 2½" (6.4cm) square Dark Pink

1 Use (2) 3" (7.6cm) squares each of White
and Pink to make (4) HST. Trim to 2½" (6.4cm)
square. Use (2) 3" (7.6cm) squares of White
and Lime Green to make (4) HST. Trim to 2½"
(6.4cm) square.

2 Paying attention to the orientation of the
connector square, connector a 2½" (6.4cm) White
square onto each side of a 2½" x 4½" (6.4cm x
11.4cm) Pink rectangle. Make (4) units.

3 Sew a Pink/White HST, a Lime Green/White HST,
and a Pink/White Connector unit together to form
a corner unit. Make (4) corner units, noting the
orientation of the units.

4 Sew together a 2½" (6.4cm) Lime Green square
and 2½" (6.4cm) Orange square. Make (4) units.

5 Sew together (4) corner units, (4) Lime Green/
Orange square units, and a 2½" (6.4cm) Dark Pink
square to form the block. Make (15) blocks.

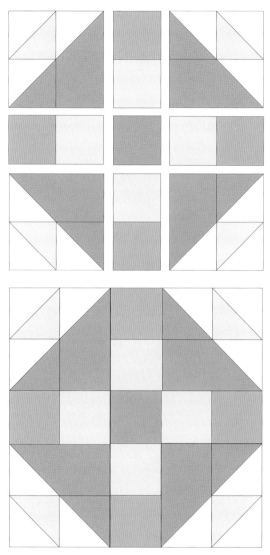

Finished Block Diagram

BLOCK 2
Finished Size: 10" (25.4cm) (Make 15)
Each block uses:
(8) 1½" (3.8cm) squares White
(12) 2½" (6.4cm) squares White
(4) 1½" (3.8cm) squares Gold
(4) 1½" (3.8cm) squares Dark Pink
(5) 2½" (6.4cm) squares Orange

1 Sew together (2) 1½" (6.4cm) White squares and
(1) 1½" (3.8cm) square each of Orange and Dark
Pink to form 2½" (6.4cm) Four Patch unit. Make
(4) Four Patch units.

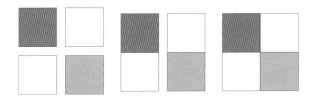

2 Sew together 2½" (6.4cm) squares of Orange,
Gold, and White to make the following units:
(2) White/Orange/White/Orange/White
(1) Gold/White/Orange/White/Gold
(2) White/Gold/White

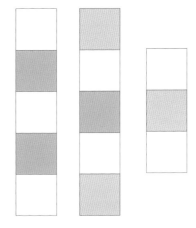

3 Add a Four Patch unit to each end of the White/
Gold/White units, noting the orientation of the
Four Patch units. Make (2) units.

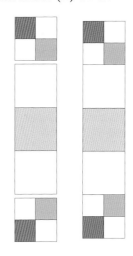

4 Referring to the Finished Block Diagram, sew
together the units to form the block. Make
(15) blocks.

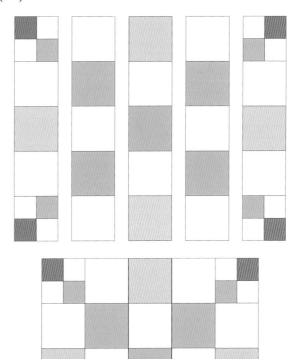

Finished Block Diagram

COMPLETE THE QUILT TOP

1 Referring to the Quilt Assembly Diagram, sew together (15) Block 1 and (15) Block 2 to complete the quilt top. The completed quilt should measure 50½" x 60½" (128.3cm x 153.7cm).

BORDERS

First Border (Lime Green)

1 Sew the 2½" (6.4cm) x WOF strips together to form a strip. From this strip, cut: (2) 2½" x 60½" (6.4cm x 153.7cm) side borders. Add (1) border strip to each side of the quilt top.

2 From the remaining strip, cut (2) 2½" x 54½" (6.4cm x 138.4cm) border strips. Referring to the First Border Diagram, add to the top and bottom of the quilt top.

Second (white) border

1 Piece together (7) 2½" (6.4cm) x WOF strips along the short edges. From this long strip, cut (2) 2½" x 64½" (6.4cm x 164cm) side borders and (2) 2½" x 54½" (6.4cm x 138.4cm) top and bottom borders. Set aside.

Third (pieced) border

1 Sew together (1) 2½" (6.4cm) x WOF strip each of Orange, Dark Pink, and Gold. Make (3) sets and cut into (40) 2½" (6.4cm) segments.

Quilt Assembly Diagram

First Border Diagram

SIDE BORDERS

1 For each side border, piece together (11) 3 color segments, then remove (1) square from one end of the borders (to make 32 squares instead of 33).

2 Sew together the 2½" x 64½" (6.4cm x 164cm) White side border and the pieced side border, noting the placement of the pieced strip and the White strip. Make 2 side borders.

3 Sew a side border to either side of the quilt top.

TOP AND BOTTOM BORDERS

1 Sew together (9) segments each for the top and bottom borders.

2 Add the 2½" x 54½" (6.4cm x 138.4cm) White strips to the pieced borders, again noting the color placement of the strips.

3 Add 4½" (11.4cm) Lime Green cornerstones to each end before adding to the quilt top.

Fourth Border (White)

1 Sew together (8) 2½" (6.4cm) x WOF White strips to form a long strip.

2 From this strip, cut (2) 2½" x 72½" (6.4cm x 184.2cm) border strips. Referring to the Pieced Border Diagram, add a border strip to each side of the quilt.

3 From the remaining strip, cut (2) 2½" x 66½" (6.4cm x 169cm) borders. Referring to the Final Border Diagram, add the borders to the top and bottom of quilt top.

FINISHING THE QUILT

1 Give the quilt top a good press. Layer and baste, then quilt as desired—we used an edge-to-edge design.

2 Bind the quilt using 2½" (6.4cm) x WOF strips. Don't forget the label!

Pieced Border Diagram

Final Border Diagram

Nostalgia

Block 1 is perfect for using up scraps from your stash. Block 2 can easily be strip pieced with leftover Jelly Roll strips.

BLOCK 1

For each block, you will need:

- **A** (1) 2½" (6.4cm) square
- **B** (4) 2½" (6.4cm) squares
- **C** (4) 2½" (6.4cm) squares
- **D** (4) 2½" x 4½" (6.4cm x 11.4cm) rectangles
- **E** (4) 2½" (6.4cm) squares
- **F** (2) 3" (7.6cm) squares for HST
- **G** (2) 3" (7.6cm) squares for HST
- **H** (2) 3" (7.6cm) squares for HST
- **I** (2) 3" (7.6cm) squares for HST

BLOCK 2

For each block, you will need:

- **A** (1) 2½ (6.4cm) square
- **B** (4) 2½" (6.4cm) squares
- **C** (4) 2½" (6.4cm) squares
- **D** (4) 2½" (6.4cm) squares
- **E** (8) 2½" (6.4cm) squares
- **F** (8) 1½" (3.8cm) squares
- **G** (8) 1½" (3.8cm) squares

BLOCK 1

BLOCK 2

Made by Anne-Marie Neumann, Freehold, NJ
Quilted by Deborah G. Stanley
Anne-Marie used her impressive stash of reproduction fabrics for this sweet homage to quilts
of the 1930s. She substituted a scrappy border for the three-fabric repeat in the original
design along with small cornerstones that repeat the color in the pieced border.

Home Sweet Home

The saturated colors of this quilt are definitely out of Linda's comfort zone, which runs to the brightest batiks. But it's good to branch out sometimes!

FABRIC REQUIREMENTS

* 3 yards (2.7m) White fabric
* ½ yard (0.5m) Light Orange fabric
* ¼ yard (0.2) Rust fabric
* ½ yard (0.5m) Teal fabric
* ⅓ yard (0.3m) Green fabric
* 1 yard (0.9m) Gold fabric
* 1⅜ yards (1.3m) Maroon fabric
* ⅛ yard (0.1m) Gray fabric
* ⅛ yard (0.1m) Gray print fabric
* ¾ yard (0.7m) Purple fabric
* ⅞ yard (0.8m) Navy fabric
* ¾ yard (0.7) Dark Orange fabric
* ⅛ yard (0.1m) Yellow fabric
* ⅓ yard (0.3m) Tan fabric
* ⅔ yard (0.6m) Binding fabric
* 5 yards (4.6m) Backing fabric (seamed vertically)
* Batting for 67" x 77" (170.2cm x 195.6cm) quilt top (twin size)

CUTTING

From the White fabric:
(20) 2½" x 5½" (6.5cm x 14cm) rectangles (Block 1)
(5) 5" (12.7cm) squares (Block 1)
(10) 4½" (11.4cm) squares (Block 1)
(40) 2½" x 4½" (6.4 x 11.4cm) rectangles (Block 2)
(40) 2½" x 8½" (6.4cm x 21.6cm) rectangles (Block 2)
(15) 2½" x (6.4cm) WOF strips (Borders 2 & 4)

From the Light Orange fabric:
(40) 2½" (6.4cm) squares (Block 2)
(2) 2½" x (6.4.cm) WOF strips (Pieced Border)

From the Rust fabric:
(20) 2½" (6.4cm) squares (Block 2)

From the Teal fabric:
(40) 2½" (6.4cm) squares (Block 2)
(2) 2½" (6.4cm) x WOF strips (Pieced Border)
(2) 2½" (6.4cm) squares (Pieced Border)

From the Green fabric:
(10) 2½" x 12½" (6.4cm x 31.8cm) rectangles (Block 1)

From the Gold fabric:
(10) 4½" x 8½" (11.4cm x 21.6cm) rectangles (Block 1)
(20) 2½" (6.4cm) squares (Block 2)
(2) 2½" (6.4cm) x WOF strips (Pieced Border)

From the Maroon fabric:
(20) 3½" x 4½" (8.9cm x 11.4cm) rectangles (Block 1)
(20) 2½" x 1½" (6.4cm x 3.8cm) rectangles (Block 1)
(10) 2½" x 2" (6.4cm x 5.1cm) rectangles (Block 1)
(10) 2½" x 4½" (6.4cm x 11.4cm) rectangles (Block 1)
(6) 2½" (6.4cm) x WOF strips (Border 1)
(2) 2½" (6.4cm) x WOF strips (Pieced Border)
(4) 4½" (11.4cm) squares (Cornerstones)

From the Gray fabric:
(10) 2½" (6.4cm) squares (Block 1)

From the Gray print fabric:
(10) 2½" x 3½" (6.4cm x 8.9cm) rectangles (Block 1)

continued on page 60

65" x 77" (165.1cm x 195.6cm)
Made and quilted by Linda J. Hahn, Palm Bay, FL
Fabric: Shadows by Banyan Batik for Northcott Silk

From the Purple fabric:
(20) 3½" x 4½" (8.9cm x 11.4cm) rectangles (Block 1)
(20) 2½" x 1½" (6.4cm x 3.8cm) rectangles (Block 1)
(10) 2½" x 2" (6.4cm x 5.1cm) rectangles (Block 1)
(10) 2½" x 4½" (6.4cm x 11.4cm) rectangles (Block 1)

From the Navy fabric:
(20) 3½" x 4½" (8.9cm x 11.4cm) rectangles (Block 1)
(20) 2½" x 1½" (6.4cm x 3.8cm) rectangles (Block 1)
(10) 2½" x 2" (6.4cm x 5.1cm) rectangles (Block 1)
(10) 2½" x 4½" (6.4cm x 11.4cm) rectangles (Block 1)
(2) 2½" (6.4cm) x WOF strips (Pieced Border)

From the Dark Orange fabric:
(20) 3½" x 4½" (8.9cm x 11.4cm) rectangles (Block 1)
(20) 2½" x 1½" (6.4cm x 3.8cm) rectangles (Block 1)
(10) 2½" x 2" (6.4cm x 5.1cm) rectangles (Block 1)
(10) 2½" x 4½" (6.4cm x 11.4cm) rectangles (Block 1)

From the Yellow fabric:
(10) 2½" x 2" (6.4cm x 5.1cm) rectangles (Block 1)

From the Tan fabric:
(5) 5" (12.7cm) squares (Block 1)
(10) 4½" (11.4cm) squares (Block 1)

From the Binding fabric:
(8) 2½" (6.4cm) x WOF strips

BLOCK 1
Finished size: 12" (30.5cm) (Make 10)
Each block uses:
(2) 2½" x 5½" rectangles White
(1) 2½" square Gray
(1) 5" square White for HST
(1) 5" square Tan for HST
(1) 4½" square Tan
(1) 4½" x 8½" rectangle Gold
(1) 4½" square White
(2) 3½" x 4½" rectangles Maroon
(2) 2½" x 1½" rectangles Maroon
(1) 2½" x 2" rectangle Maroon
(1) 2½" x 4½" rectangle Maroon
(1) 2½" x 2" rectangle Yellow
(1) 2½" x 3½" rectangle Gray Print
(1) 2½" x 12½" rectangle Green

Chimney Section:
1 Sew (2) 2½" x 5½" (6.4cm x 14cm) White rectangles to (1) 2½" (6.4cm) Gray square.

Roof Section:
1 Sew together (1) 5" (12.7cm) square each of Tan and White to make an HST. Trim to 4½" (11.4cm) square.

2 Add a 4½" (11.4cm) white connector to the left of a 4½" x 8½" (11.4cm x 21.6cm) Gold rectangle. Add a 4½" (6.4cm) connector to the right of the unit, noting the orientation of the connectors.

3 Sew together a Tan/White HST and a Tan/Gold/White connector unit to form the roof.

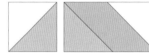

House Section:
1 Sew together the 2½" x 3½" (6.4cm x 8.9cm) rectangle Gray and 2½" x 1½" (6.4cm x 3.8cm) Maroon rectangle to form the Door section.

2 Sew together (1) each of the following: 2½" x 1½" (6.4cm x 3.8cm) Maroon rectangle, 2½" x 2" (6.4cm x 5.1cm) Yellow rectangle and 2½" x 2" (6.4cm x 5.1cm) Maroon rectangle to form a Window section.

3 Sew together one each of the following: 3½" x 4½" (8.9cm x 11.4cm) Maroon rectangle, Door section, 3½" x 4½" (8.9cm x 11.4cm) Maroon rectangle, Window section and 2½" x 4½" (6.4cm x 11.4cm) Maroon rectangle to form the House section.

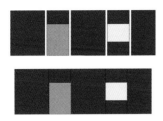

4 Sew together the Chimney section, the Roof section and the House section. Add a 2½" x 12½" (6.4cm x 31.8cm) Green rectangle to the bottom of the block. Repeat the steps to make a second Maroon House block.

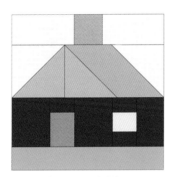

Finished Block Diagram

5 Make (2) House blocks each in Purple, Navy, Dark Orange, and Teal, keeping the roof, door, window and chimney fabrics the same in each block.

BLOCK 2
Finished size 12" (30.5cm) (Make 10)
Each block uses:
(4) 2½" (6.4cm) squares Light Orange
(2) 2½" (6.4cm) squares Gold
(4) 2½" x 4½" (6.4cm x 11.4cm) rectangles White
(4) 2½" x 8½" (6.4cm x 21.6cm) rectangles White
(2) 2½" (6.4cm) squares Rust
(4) 2½" (6.4cm) squares Teal

1 Sew together (2) 2½" (6.4cm) Light Orange squares and (2) 2½" (6.4cm) Rust squares to make a Four Patch unit.

2 Stitch (1) 2½" x 4½" (6.4cm x 11.4cm) White rectangle onto opposite sides of the Four Patch unit. Be sure to maintain the position of the Light Orange and Rust Four Patch unit.

3 Stitch a 2½" (6.4cm) Teal square on each end of a 2½" x 4½" (6.4cm x 11.4cm) White rectangle. Make (2) units.

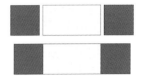

4 Attach the Teal/White/Teal units to the Four Patch units.

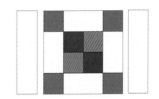 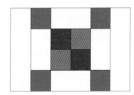

5 Sew (2) 2½" x 8½" (6.4cm x 21.6cm) White rectangles to opposite sides of the Light Orange/Rust/Teal unit.

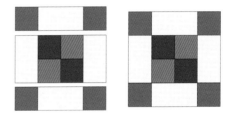

6 Sew (1) 2½" (6.4cm) Gold square and (1) 2½" (6.4cm) Light Orange square to opposite ends of a 2½"x 8½" (6.4cm x 21.6cm) White rectangle. Make (2) units.

7 Sew a Gold/White/Light Orange unit to the top and bottom of the Light Orange/Rust/Teal/White unit to complete the block, noting the placement of the Gold and Orange squares.

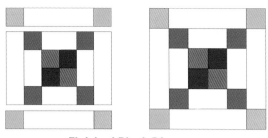

Finished Block Diagram

8 Repeat steps to make (10) blocks.

COMPLETE QUILT TOP
Referring to diagram, sew together (10) Block 1 and (10) Block, alternating the blocks as shown. The completed quilt should measure 48½" x 60½" (123.2cm x 153.7cm).

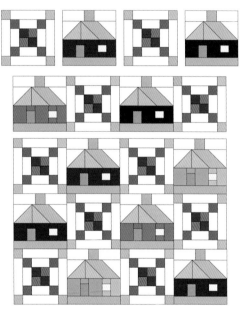

Quilt Assembly Diagram

BORDERS
First Border (Maroon)
1 Sew together (6) 2½" (6.4cm) x WOF Maroon strips to form a long strip.

2 From the strip, cut (2) 2½" x 60½" (6.4cm x 153.7cm) side borders. Add the side borders to the sides of the quilt top.

3 From the remaining strip, cut (2) 2½" x 52½" (6.4cm x 134.4cm) border strips. Add the strips to the top and bottom of the quilt top.

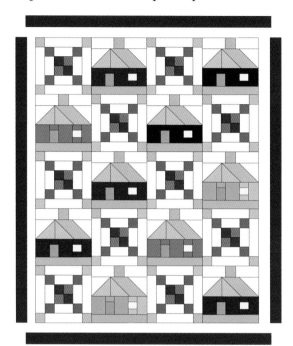

First Border Diagram

Second (white) border
1 Piece together (7) 2½" (6.4cm) x WOF White strips along the short edges.

2 From this long strip, cut (2) 2½" x 64½" (6.4cm x 164cm) side borders and (2) 2½" x 52½" (6.4cm x 133.4cm) top and bottom borders from the White background fabric. Set aside.

Third (pieced) border
1 Make (2) strip sets. Sew together (1) 2½" (6.4cm) x WOF strip each of Teal, Light Orange, Maroon, Gold and Navy.

2 Make (2) strip sets. Cut each strip set into (24) 2½" (6.4cm) segments.

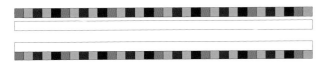

Side Borders

1 For each side border, piece together (7) 5 color segments. Remove (3) 2½" (6.4cm) squares from one end of the strip to form a 32-square strip.

2 Sew together the 2½" x 64½" (6.4cm x 164cm) White side border and the pieced side border. Repeat steps to create a second side border. Add to the sides of the quilt top.

Top and Bottom Borders

1 Sew together (5) segments each for the top and bottom borders.

2 Add (1) 2½" (6.4cm) Teal square to one end of the strip.

3 Add the 2½" x 52½" (6.4cm x 133.4cm) White strips to the pieced borders.

4 Sew a 4½" (6.4cm) Maroon cornerstone to each end before adding to the quilt top.

Pieced Border Diagram

Fourth Border (White)

1 Sew together (8) 2½" (6.4cm) x WOF White strips to form a long strip.

2 From this strip, cut (2) 2½" x 72½" (6.4cm x 184.2cm) border strips. Add the strips to the sides of the quilt top.

3 From the remainder, cut (2) 2 ½" x 64 ½" (6.4cm x 164cm) borders. Add to the top and bottom of the quilt top.

FINISHING THE QUILT

1 Give the quilt top a good press, then layer and baste. Quilt as desired—we used an edge-to-edge design.

2 Bind the quilt using 2½" (6.4cm) x WOF strips. Don't forget the label!

Final Border Diagram

Home Is Where the Food Is

Block 1 is perfect for using up scraps from your stash. Block 2 can easily be strip pieced with leftover Jelly Roll strips.

BLOCK 1

For each block, you will need:

- **A** (2) 2½" x 5½" (6.4cm x 14cm) rectangles
- **B** (1) 2½" (6.4cm) square
- **C** (1) 5" (12.7cm) square for HST
- **D** (1) 5" (12.7cm) square for HST
- **E** (1) 4½" (11.4cm) square
- **F** (1) 4½" x 8½" (11.4cm x 21.6cm) rectangle
- **G** (1) 4½" (11.4cm) square
- **H** (2) 3½" x 4½" (8.9cm x 11.4cm) rectangles
- **I** (2) 2½" x 1½" (6.4cm x 3.8cm) rectangles
- **J** (1) 2½" x 3½" (6.4cm x 8.9cm) rectangle
- **K** (1) 2½" x 2" (6.4cm x 5.1cm) rectangle
- **L** (1) 2½" x 2" (6.4ccm x 5.1cm) rectangle
- **M** (1) 2½" x 4½" (6.4cm x 11.4cm) rectangle
- **N** (1) 2½" x 12½" (6.4cm x 31.8cm) rectangle

BLOCK 2

For each block, you will need:

- **A** (2) 2½" (6.4cm) squares
- **B** (2) 2½" (6.4cm) squares
- **C** (4) 2½" (6.4cm) squares
- **D** (4) 2½" x 4½" (6.4cm x 11.4cm) rectangles
- **E** (4) 2½" x 8½" (6.4cm x 21.6cm) rectangles
- **F** (4) 2½" (6.4cm) squares

BLOCK 1

BLOCK 2

Made by Stevii Thompson Graves, Leesburg, VA
Quilted by Linda J. Hahn, Palm Bay, FL
Stevii used lots of different food-themed novelty prints—from blueberries and
strawberries to pretzels and pizza—to create this whimsical quilt. She even
embellished the top with beaded doorknobs after it was quilted.

BOTANICAL QUILTS

Lavender Sachet

The soft purple palette of this quilt was inspired by Deb's grandmother's hope chest, which occupies a place of honor in her home.

FABRIC REQUIREMENTS

- 2 yards (1.8m) White fabric
- 1¾ yards (1.6m) Tan fabric
- 1¼ yards (1.1m) Light Purple fabric
- ¾ yard (0.7m) Medium Purple fabric
- 1¼ yards (1.1m) Dark Purple fabric
- ⅝ yard (0.6m) Binding fabric
- 4 yards (3.7m) Backing fabric (seamed vertically)
- Batting for 61" x 61" (155m) quilt top (twin size)

CUTTING

From the White fabric:
(156) 2½" (6.4cm) squares (Block 1)
(13) 4½" (6.4cm) squares (Block 1)
(52) 2½" x 4½" (6.4cm x 11.4cm) rectangles (Block 1)
(24) 4" (11.4cm) squares (Block 2)

From the Tan fabric:
(26) 3" (7.6cm) squares (Block 1)
(52) 2½" x 4½" (6.4cm x 11.4cm) rectangles (Block 1)
(24) 4" (11.4cm) squares (Block 2)
(12) 5" (12.7cm) squares (Block 2)
(24) 2½" (6.4cm) squares (Block 2)

From the Light Purple fabric:
(52) 2½" x 4½" (6.4cm x 11.4cm) rectangles (Block 1)
(104) 2½" (6.4cm) squares (Block 1)

From the Medium Purple fabric:
(48) 2½" x 4½" (6.4cm x 11.4cm) rectangles (Block 2)
(24) 3½" (6.4cm) squares (Block 2)

From the Dark Purple fabric:
(26) 3" squares (7.6cm) (Block 1)
(52) 2½" (6.4cm) squares (Block 1)
(12) 5" squares (12.7cm) (Block 2)
(24) 3½" (8.9cm) squares (Block 2)

From the Binding fabric:
(7) 2½" (6.4cm) x WOF strips

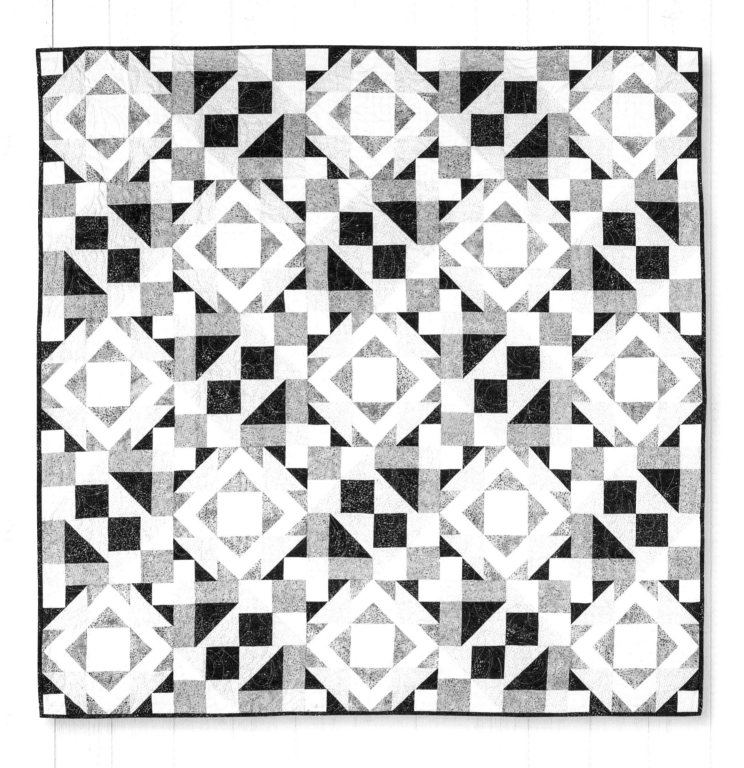

61" (155cm) Square
Made by Anne-Marie Neumann, Freehold, NJ. Quilted by Deborah G. Stanley, Matawan, NJ
Fabric Collection: Ketan from Banyan Batiks by Northcott Silk

BLOCK 1
Finished size: 12" (30.5cm) (Make 13)
Each block uses:
(12) 2½" (6.4cm) squares White
(4) 2½" x 4½" (6.4cm x 11.4cm) White rectangles
(1) 4½" (11.4cm) White square
(2) 3" (7.6cm) squares Tan for HST
(4) 2½" x 4½" (6.4cm x 11.4cm) rectangles Tan
(4) 2½" x 4½" (6.4cm x 11.4cm) rectangles
    Light Purple
(8) 2½" (6.4cm) squares Light Purple
(2) 3" (7.6cm) Dark Purple squares for HST
(4) 2½" (6.4cm) squares Dark Purple

1 Use (2) 3" (7.6cm) squares of Tan and
Dark Purple to make (4) HST. Trim to 2½"
(6.4cm) square.

2 Paying attention to the orientation of the connector
square, connector a 2½" (6.4cm) Dark Purple square
onto each side of a 2½" x 4½" (6.4cm x 11.4cm)
Tan rectangle. Make (4) units.

3 Sew together a Tan/Dark Purple HST, a 2½"
(6.4cm) White square, and a Tan/Dark Purple
Connector unit to form a corner unit. Make (4)
corner units. Pay attention to the orientation of
the units.

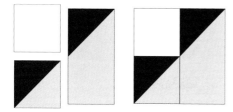

4 Sew a 2½" (6.4cm) White square onto each side of
a 2½" x 4½" (6.4cm x 11.4cm) Light Purple rectangle
to form a Flying Geese unit. Repeat using a 2½" x 4½"
(6.4cm x 11.4cm) White rectangle and 2½" (6.4cm)
Light Purple squares. Sew the Flying Geese units
together, with the Light Purple/White unit on the
bottom, to form a side unit. Make (4) side units.

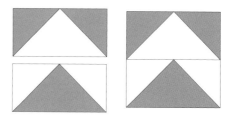

5 Sew together the corner units, side units and a 4½"
(11.4cm) White center square to form the block.
Make (13) blocks.

Finished Block Diagram

BLOCK 2
Finished size: 12" (30.5cm) (make 12)
Each block uses:
(2) 4" (6.4cm) squares White for HST
(2) 4" (6.4cm) squares Tan for HST
(1) 5" (12.7cm) square Tan for HST
(2) 2½" (6.4cm) squares Tan
(4) 2½" x 4½" (6.4cm x 11.4cm) rectangles
    Medium Purple
(2) 3½" (9.9cm) squares Medium Purple
(1) 5" (12.7cm) square Dark Purple for HST
(2) 3½" (8.9cm) squares Dark Purple

1 Use 4" (11.4cm) squares of White and Tan to make (4) HST. Trim to 3½" (8.9cm) square.

2 Sew together (1) 3½" (8.9cm) Medium Purple square, (2) HST units and (1) 3½" (8.9cm) Dark Purple square, noting the orientation of the squares and HST units. Make (4) corner units.

3 Use 5" (12.7cm) squares of White and Purple to make (4) HST. Trim to 4½" (11.4cm) square.

4 Add (2) 2½" x 4½" (6.4cm x 11.4cm) Medium Purple rectangles and (1) 2½" (6.4cm) Tan square to the Purple/Tan HST unit, noting the orientation of the units. Make (4) corner units.

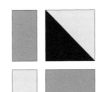

5 Sew together the units to form a block, paying attention to the orientation of the units. Make (12) blocks.

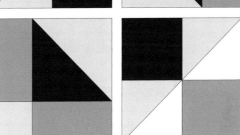

Finished Block Diagram

COMPLETE QUILT TOP:

1 Sew together (13) Block 1 and (12) Block 2, alternating the blocks, to complete the quilt top. The completed quilt should measure 60½" (153.7cm) square.

FINISHING THE QUILT

1 Give the quilt top a good press. Layer and baste. Quilt as desired—we used an edge-to-edge design.

2 Bind the quilt using 2½" (6.4cm) x WOF strips. Don't forget the label!

Quilt Assembly Diagram

Deb used light purple thread and an edge-to-edge feather pantograph from Urban Elementz for the surface quilting.

Evergreen

Use what you have to make each block a different color. Keep the values as they are or change things up!

BLOCK 1

For each block, you will need:

- **A** (1) 4½" (11.4cm) square
- **B** (4) 2½" x 4½" (6.4cm x 11.4cm) rectangles
- **C** (8) 2½" (6.4cm) squares
- **D** (4) 2½" x 4½" (6.4cm x 11.4cm) rectangles
- **E** (8) 2½" (6.4cm) squares
- **F** (4) 2½" x 4½" (6.4cm x 11.4cm) rectangles
- **G** (4) 2½" (6.4cm) squares
- **H** (2) 3" (7.6cm) squares for HST
- **I** (2) 3" (7.6cm) squares for HST
- **J** (4) 2½" (6.4cm) squares

BLOCK 2

For each block, you will need:

- **A** (2) 3½" (7.6cm) squares
- **B** (2) 4" (11.4cm) squares for HST
- **C** (2) 4" (11.4cm) squares for HST
- **D** (2) 3½" (8.9cm) squares
- **E** (1) 5" (12.7cm) square for HST
- **F** (1) 5" (12.7cm) square for HST
- **G** (4) 2½" x 4½" (6.4cm x 11.4cm) rectangles
- **H** (2) 2½" (6.4cm) squares

BLOCK 1

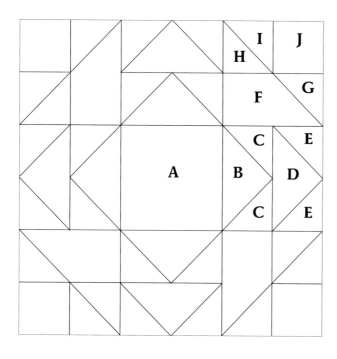

BLOCK 2

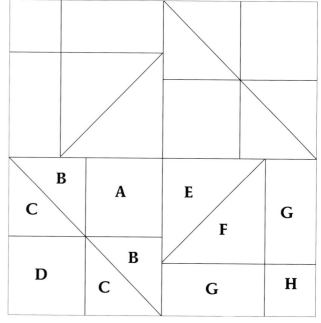

Made by Levi Henson, Cruso, NC
Quilted by Deborah G. Stanley, Matawan, NJ
Levi used clear batiks from his stash to create this red and green quilt that
is appropriate for the holidays, but could be used year-round!

Fields of Green

Many shades and patterns of green make up this lively quilt. The wide sashing adds an additional design element.

FABRIC REQUIREMENTS

* ¼ yard (0.2m) White fabric
* ⅝ yard (0.6m) Black fabric
* ½ yard (0.5m) Light Green fabric
* 1½ yards (1.4m) Bright Green fabric
* ⅛ yard (0.1m) Dark Green fabric
* ½ yard (0.5m) Medium Green fabric
* 1 yard (0.9m) Lime Green fabric
* ¾ yards (0.7m) Yellow-Green fabric
* 1¼ yards (1.1m) Darkest Green fabric
* ⅝ yard (0.6m) Binding fabric
* 4 yards (3.7m) Backing fabric (seamed vertically)
* Batting for 56" (142.2cm) square quilt top (twin size)

CUTTING

From the White fabric:
(40) 2" (6.4cm) squares (Block 1)

From the Black fabric:
(40) 2" (5.1cm) squares (Block 1)
(32) 2½" (6.4cm) squares (Block 2)
(16) 3" (7.6cm) squares (Block 2)

From the Light Green fabric:
(80) 3½" x 2" (8.9cm x 5.1cm) (Block 1)

From the Bright Green fabric:
(160) 2" (5.1cm) squares (Block 1)
(16) 2½" (6.4cm) squares (Block 2)
(32) 3½" x 6½" (8.9cm x 16.5cm) (Sashing)
(4) 2½" (6.4cm) squares (Border cornerstones)

From the Dark Green fabric:
(8) 3½" (8.9cm) squares (Block 1)

From the Medium Green fabric:
(4) 3½" (8.9cm) squares (Block 1)
(32) 2½" (6.4cm) squares (Block 2)
(24) 3" (7.6cm) squares (Block 2)

From the Lime Green fabric:
(8) 3½" (8.9cm) squares (Block 1)
(16) 2½" (6.4cm) squares (Block 2)
(4) 3½" x 6½" (8.9cm x 16.5cm) rectangles (Sashing)
(4) 1½" (3.8cm) x WOF strips (Sashing)
(5) 2½" (6.4cm) x WOF strips (Border)

From the Yellow-Green fabric:
(24) 3½" x 6½" (8.9cm x 16.5cm) rectangles (Sashing)
(8) 3" (7.6cm) squares (Block 2)

From the Darkest Green fabric:
(240) 2" (5.1cm) squares (Sashing)
(5) 1½" (3.8cm) x WOF strips (Sashing)

From the Binding fabric:
(7) 2½" (6.4cm) x WOF strips

56" (142.4cm) Square
Made and quilted by Deborah G. Stanley, Matawan, NJ
Fabric: Ketan and Shadows collections by Banyan Batiks for Northcott Silk

BLOCK 1
Finished size: 6" (16.5cm) (Make 20)
Each block uses:
(4) 2" x 3½" (5.1cm x 8.9cm) rectangles
   Light Green
(8) 2" (5.1cm) squares Bright Green
(1) 3½" (8.9cm) Center Square (Lime Green,
   Medium Green, Dark Green)
(2) 2" (5.1cm) squares Black
(2) 2" (5.1cm) squares White

1 Paying attention to the orientation of the
connector square, connector a 2" (5.1cm) Bright
Green square onto either side of a 2" x 3½" (5.1cm
x 8.9cm) Light Green rectangle. Make (4) units.

2 Sew together (4) connector units, (1) 3½"
(8.9cm) center square, (2) 2" (5.1cm) Black
squares and (2) 2" (5.1cm) White squares to form
the block.

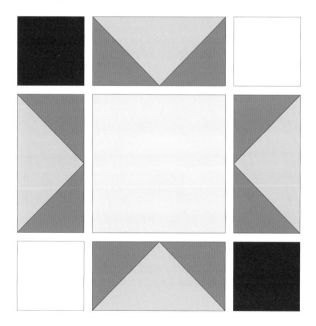

3 In the same manner as step 2, create
the following:
(8) blocks with a Lime Green center
(8) blocks with a Dark Green center
(4) blocks with a Medium Green center

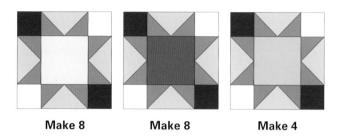

Make 8   **Make 8**   **Make 4**

BLOCK 2
Finished size: 6" (15.2cm) (Make 16)
Each block uses:
(2) 2½" (6.4cm) squares Medium Green
(2) 3" (7.6cm) square Medium Green for HST
(1) 2½" (6.4cm) square Lime Green
(1) 3" (7.6cm) square Yellow-Green for HST
(1) 2½" (6.4cm) square Bright Green
(2) 2½" (6.4cm) squares Black
(1) 3" (7.6cm) square Black for HST

1 Use 3" (7.6cm) squares of Medium Green, Black,
and Medium Yellow to make HST units. Trim to 2½"
(6.4cm) square. Make (2) Medium Green/Black
HST and (1) Medium Green/Yellow-Green.

2 Referring to the Finished Block Diagram, stitch together the Yellow Green/Medium Green HST, (2) Black/Medium Green HST, (2) 2½" (6.4cm) Medium Green squares, a Black, and a Lime Green to form the block. Note the orientation of the squares and HST.

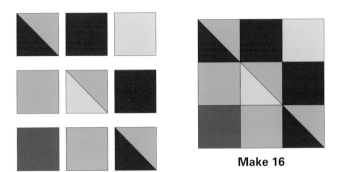

Make 16

Finished Block Diagram

SASHING UNITS

1 Connector 2" (6.4cm) squares Darkest Green onto all four sides of a 3½" x 6½" (8.9cm x 16.5cm) Yellow-Green rectangle.

2 Repeat to make a total of (60) blocks in the following combinations, using Darkest Green connectors on all blocks:
Make (24) Yellow-Green
Make (4) Lime Green
Make (32) Bright Green

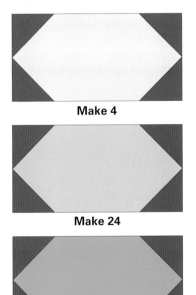

Make 4

Make 24

Make 32

SASHING NINE PATCH UNITS

1 Sew together (2) 1½" (3.8cm) x WOF Lime Green strips and (1) 1½" (3.9cm) x WOF Darkest Green strip to form a 3 row strip set. Cut the strip into (25) 1½" (3.8cm) segments.

Sew together (2) 1½" (3.8cm) x WOF Darkest Green strips and (1) 1½" (3.8cm) x WOF Lime Green strip. Make (2) strip sets. Cut the strip sets into (50) 1½" (3.8cm) segments.

3 Combine segments to form a 3½" (8.9cm) Nine Patch unit. Make (25) units.

Make 25

COMPLETE QUILT TOP

1 Sew together the blocks and sashing units to form the first row, noting the orientation of the Split Nine Patch units and placement of various colorings of Star Blocks and Sashing Units.

2 Continue to form rows using Block 1 and Block 2, Sashing units and Sashing Nine Patch units, being mindful of color placement and orientation. Sew the rows together to form the quilt top.

BORDERS

Refer to page 15 for instructions on adding borders.

1 Sew together 2½" x WOF strips to form a long strip. From this strip, cut (4) 2½" x 51½" (6.4cm x 131cm) strips.

2 Sew a border strip to either side of the quilt top.

3 Add a 2½" (6.4cm) Bright Green square to each end of the remaining border strips.

4 Add the strips to the top and bottom of the quilt top.

FINISHING THE QUILT

1 Give the quilt top a good press. Layer and baste. Quilt as desired—we used an edge-to-edge design.

2 Bind the quilt using 2½" (6.4cm) x WOF strips. Don't forget the label!

Quilt Assembly Diagram

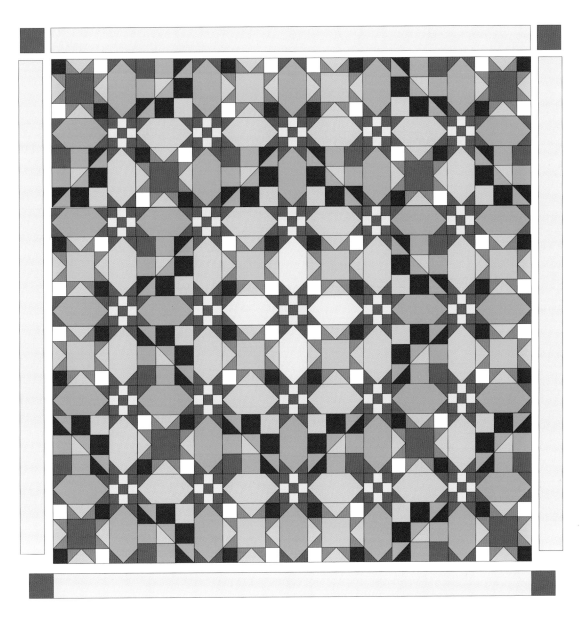

Border Assembly Diagram

Queen of the Rodeo

Play around with the color in these blocks. Try these blocks in a quilt-design program (we use Electric Quilt) or go old-school with photocopies of the blocks and colored pencils!

BLOCK 1

For each block, you will need:

- **A** (1) 3½" (8.9cm) Center Square
- **B** (4) 2" x 3½" (5.1cm x 8.9cm) rectangles
- **C** (8) 2" (5.1cm) squares
- **D** (2) 2" (5.1cm) squares
- **E** (2) 2" (5.1cm) squares

BLOCK 2

For each block, you will need:

- **A** (1) 2½" (6.4cm) square
- **B** (2) 2½" (6.4cm) squares
- **C** (2) 3" (8.9cm) square for HST
- **D** (1) 3" (8.9cm) square for HST
- **E** (1) 3" (8.9cm) square for HST
- **F** (2) 2½" (6.4cm) squares
- **G** (1) 2½" (6.4cm) square

BLOCK 1

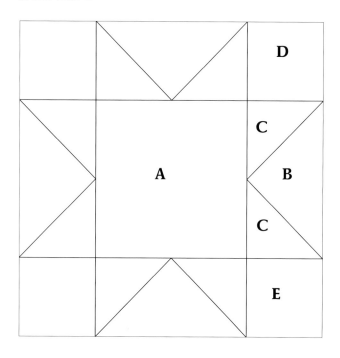

BLOCK 2

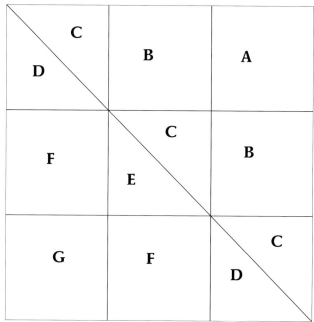

Made by Rebecca Szabo, Howell, NJ. Quilted by Deborah G. Stanley, Matawan, NJ
Rebecca used a wide assortment of novelty prints, many cowboy-themed, for
this quilt, and added a pieced border to use up the leftover fabric! Fun Fact:
Linda used to be a barrel racer in the rodeo circuit years ago!

Party Time

This design was inspired by Linda's second fabric collection for Banyan Batiks. It incorporates Deb's favorites from the collection, including this awesome stripe!

FABRIC REQUIREMENTS

- 2¾ yards (2.5m) White fabric
- ½ yard (0.5m) Green Swirl fabric
- ½ yard (0.5m) Green Dot fabric
- ⅜ yard (0.3m) Dark Green fabric
- ⅜ yard (0.3m) Pink Swirl fabric
- ⅜ yard (0.3m) Coral Swirl fabric
- ⅜ yard (0.3m) Multi-swirl fabric
- ¼ yard (0.2m) Turquoise fabric
- ¼ yard (0.2m) Orange Dot fabric
- ⅜ yard (0.3m) Stripe fabric (allow ½ yard [0.5m] if fussy cutting)
- ⅝ yard (0.6m) Binding fabric
- 4 yards (3.7m) Backing fabric (seamed vertically)
- Batting for 61" x 61" (155cm) quilt top (twin size)

CUTTING

From the White fabric:
(260) 2½" (6.4cm) squares
(26) 3" (7.6cm) squares for HST
(4) 14" (35.6cm) squares cut once on diagonal
(1) 14" (35.6cm) square cut twice on the diagonal

From the Green Swirl fabric:
(26) 2½" x 4½" (6.4cm x 11.4cm) rectangles
(13) 3" (7.6cm) squares for HST

From the Green Dot fabric:
(26) 2½" x 4½" (6.4cm x 11.4cm) rectangles
(13) 3" (7.6cm) squares for HST

From the Dark Green fabric:
(26) 2½" x 4½" (6.4cm x 11.4cm) rectangles

From the Pink Swirl fabric:
(26) 2½" x 4½" (6.4cm x 11.4cm) rectangles

From the Coral Swirl:
(26) 2½" x 4½" (6.4cm x 11.4cm) rectangles

From the Multi-swirl:
(26) 2½" x 4½" (6.4cm x 11.4cm) rectangles

From the Turquoise swirl:
(26) 2½" (6.4cm) squares

From the Orange Dot fabric:
(26) 2½" (6.4cm) squares

From the Stripe fabric:
(13) 4½" (6.4cm) squares (for this quilt, these were fussy cut to align the stripe)

61" (155cm) Square
Made and quilted by Deborah G. Stanley, Matawan, NJ
This design was inspired by Linda's second fabric collection for Banyan Batiks. It incorporates Deb's favorites from the collection, including this awesome stripe!
Fabric: Carnivale from Banyan Batiks by Northcott Silk

BLOCK 1
Finished size 12" (30.5cm) (make 13)
Each block uses:
(20) 2½" (6.4cm) squares White
(2) 3" (7.6cm) square White
(2) 2½" x 4½" (6.4cm x 11.4cm) rectangles
  Green Swirl
(1) 3" (7.6cm) square Green Swirl for HST
(2) 2½" x 4½" (6.4cm x 11.4cm) rectangles
  Green Dot
(1) 3" (7.6cm) square Green Dot
(1) 4½" (11.4cm) square Stripe
(2) 2½" x 4½" (6.4cm x 11.4cm) rectangles
  Dark Green
(2) 2½" x 4½" (6.4cm x 11.4cm) rectangles
  Pink Swirl
(2) 2½" x 4½" (6.4cm x 11.4cm) rectangles
  Coral Swirl
(2) 2½" x 4½" (6.4cm x 11.4cm) rectangles
  Multi-swirl

1 Use 3" (7.6cm) squares of Green Swirl and
White to make (2) HST. Trim to 2½" (6.4cm)
square. Repeat using 3" (7.6cm) squares of Green
Dot and White to make (2) HST. Trim to 2½"
(6.4cm) square.

2 Paying attention to the orientation of the
connector square, connector a 2½" (6.4cm) White
square onto one side of a 2½" x 4½" (6.4cm x
11.4cm) Green Swirl rectangle. Repeat to make (2)
Green Swirl/White units. Make (2) more units
using Green Dot rectangles and 2½" (6.4cm)
White squares.

3 Sew together a Green Swirl/White HST, 2½"
(6.4cm) Turquoise square, and a Green Swirl/White
connector unit to form corner unit. Make 2 units.
Make (2) more corner units using Green Dot/White
HST, Green Dot/White connector units, and 2½"
(6.4cm) Orange Dot squares. Pay attention to the
orientation of the units.

4 Sew a 2½" (6.4cm) White square onto either
side of a 2½" x 4½" (6.4cm x 11.4cm) Dark Green
rectangle to form a Flying Geese unit. Make 2 units.
Repeat using 2½" (6.4cm) White squares and
2½" x 4½" (6.4cm x 11.4cm) rectangles of Pink
Swirl, Coral Swirl, and Multi-swirl. Make (2) of
each combination.

  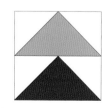

5 Sew together (4) corner units, (4) side units, and a 4½" (11.4cm) Stripe center square to form the block. Be sure that the stripe, if using, is positioned in the same direction for all blocks. Make (13) blocks.

Finished Block Diagram

COMPLETE QUILT TOP

1 Sew (13) blocks together with triangles cut from 14" (35.6cm) squares to complete the quilt top. Add the quarter-square triangles to the top and sides as indicated. We recommended trimming the quilt AFTER quilting. Be sure to leave ¼" (6mm) seam allowance beyond the turquoise and orange squares to allow for the binding to be attached without cutting off the points. The completed quilt should measure about 60½" (154cm) square after trimming.

FINISHING THE QUILT

1 Give the quilt top a good press. Layer and baste. Quilt as desired. We used an edge-to-edge design.

2 Bind the quilt using 2½" (6.4cm) x WOF strips. Don't forget the label!

Quilt Assembly Diagram

Note: All triangles are bigger than needed for ease of construction.

Neutral Ground

This block is perfect for using up partial jelly-roll strips—
make each of the flying geese a different color!

BLOCK 1

For each block, you will need:

- **A** (1) 4½" (11.4cm) square
- **B** (4) 2½" x 4½" (6.4cm x 11.4cm) rectangles
- **C** (8) 2½" (6.4cm) squares
- **D** (4) 2½" x 4½" (6.4cm x 11.4cm) rectangles
- **E** (8) 2½" (6.4cm) squares
- **F** (4) 2½" x 4½" (6.4cm x 11.4cm) rectangles
- **G** (4) 2½" (6.4cm) squares
- **H** (2) 3" (7.6cm) squares for HST
- **I** (2) 3" (7.6cm) squares for HST
- **J** (4) 2½" (6.4cm) squares

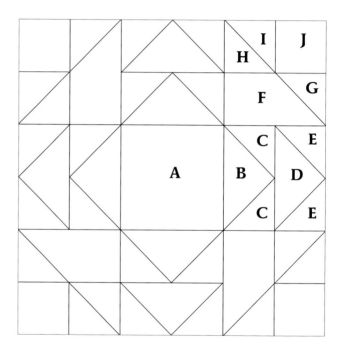

Made and quilted by Deborah G. Stanley, Matawan, NJ
Deb used fabrics from her stash of Japanese taupes and neutrals to
complete this wall-hanging version of the original quilt design.

Rainbow Collection

Simplicity is the keyword for this quilt. Clean lines and a limited palette of solid colors give this quilt a soothing quality.

FABRIC REQUIREMENTS

- ❋ 1 yard (0.9m) Dark Blue fabric
- ❋ 2¼ yards White fabric
- ❋ ¼ yard (0.2m) Pink fabric
- ❋ ⅓ yard (0.3m) Coral fabric
- ❋ ⅓ yard (0.3m) Medium Blue fabric
- ❋ ⅓ yard (0.3m) Gold fabric
- ❋ ⅓ yard (0.3m) Teal fabric
- ❋ ⅓ yard (0.3m) Green fabric
- ❋ ⅓ (0.3m) Yellow fabric
- ❋ ⅝ yard (0.6m) Binding fabric
- ❋ 4 yards Backing fabric (seamed vertically)
- ❋ Batting for 51" x 67" (130cm x 170.2cm) quilt top (twin size)

CUTTING

From the Dark Blue fabric:
- (36) 3½" (8.9cm) squares (Block 1)
- (12) 3½" x 6½" (8.9cm x 16.5cm) rectangles (Block 1)
- (6) 4½" (6.4cm) squares cut twice on the diagonal (Block 1)
- (8) 3½" (8.9cm) squares (Block 2)

From the White fabric:
- (8) 3½" (8.9cm) squares (Block 2)
- (2) 7" (17.8cm) squares for HST (Block 2)
- (3) 10" (25.4cm) squares cut once on the diagonal
- (6) 8½" (21.6cm) x WOF strips (Border)

From the Pink fabric:
- (6) 4½" (11.4cm) squares cut twice on the diagonal (Block 1)

From the Coral fabric:
- (2) 3½" (8.9cm) squares (Block 1)
- (2) 4½" (11.4cm) squares cut twice on the diagonal (Block 1)
- (1) 7" (17.9cm) square for HST (Block 2)
- (1) 10" (25.4cm) square cut once on the diagonal

From the Medium Blue fabric:
- (2) 3½" (8.9cm) squares (Block 1)
- (2) 4½" (11.4cm) squares cut twice on the diagonal (Block 1)
- (1) 7" (17.8cm) square for HST (Block 2)
- (1) 10" (25.4cm) square cut once on the diagonal

From the Gold fabric:
- (2) 3½" (8.9cm) squares (Block 1)
- (2) 4½" (11.4cm) squares cut twice on the diagonal (Block 1)
- (1) 7" (17.8cm) square for HST (Block 2)
- (1) 10" (25.4cm) square cut once on the diagonal

From the Teal fabric:
- (2) 3½" (8.9cm) squares (Block 1)
- (2) 4½" (11.4cm) squares cut twice on the diagonal (Block 1)
- (1) 7" (17.8cm) square for HST (Block 2)
- (1) 10" (25.4cm) square cut once on the diagonal

continued on page 90

51" x 67" (130cm x 170.2cm)
Made and quilted by Deborah G. Stanley, Matawan, NJ
Fabric: Assorted Solids

From the Green fabric:
(2) 3½" (8.9cm) squares (Block 1)
(2) 4½" (11.4cm) squares cut twice on the diagonal (Block 1)
(1) 7" (17.8cm) square for HST (Block 2)
(2) 10" (25.4cm) squares cut once on the diagonal

From the Yellow fabric:
(2) 3½" (8.9cm) squares (Block 1)
(2) 4½" (11.4cm) squares cut twice on the diagonal (Block 1)
(1) 7" (17.8cm) square for HST (Block 2)
(2) 10" (25.4cm) squares cut once on the diagonal

From the Binding fabric:
(7) 2½" (6.4cm) x WOF strips

BLOCK 1
Finished size: 12" (Make 6)

Each block uses:
(6) 3½" (8.9cm) squares Dark Blue
(2) 3½" x 6½" (8.9cm x 16.5cm) rectangles Dark Blue
(1) 4½" (11.4cm) square Dark Blue cut twice on the diagonal
(1) 4½" (11.4cm) square Pink cut twice on the diagonal
(2) 3½" (8.9cm) squares Coral
(2) 4½" (11.4cm) squares Coral, cut twice on the diagonal

1 Sew together (2) Coral triangles, a Dark Blue triangle and a Pink triangle to form a Star Point unit. Trim to 3½" (8.9cm) square. Make (4) star point units.

2 Sew together (4) Star Point units with (5) 3½" (8.9cm) Dark Blue squares to form a Star Unit.

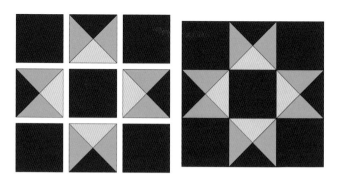

3 Sew together (1) 3½" x 6½" (8.9cm x 16.5cm) Dark Blue rectangle and (1) 3½" (8.9cm) Coral square. Make (2) units.

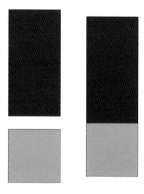

4 Sew one unit to the side of the Star unit, noting the orientation of the Coral square.

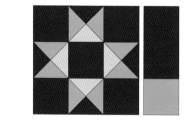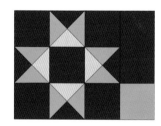

5 Sew (1) 3½" (8.9cm) Dark Blue square to the remaining Coral/Dark Blue unit. Add to the bottom of the star unit. Make a Star block in each colorway: Coral, Medium Blue, Teal, Yellow, Green and Gold. Make (6) blocks total.

Finished Block Diagram

BLOCK 2
Finished size: 12" (30.5cm) (Make 2 blocks, one of each combination)
Each block uses:
(4) 3½" (8.9cm) White squares
(4) 3½" (8.9cm) Dark Blue squares
(1) 7" (17.8cm) White square
(1) 7" (17.8cm) Gold square
(1) 7" (17.8cm) Medium Blue square
(1) 7" (17.8cm) Coral square

1 Use the 7" (17.8cm) squares to make HST units. Trim to 6½" (16.5cm) square. Make (1) Coral/Medium Blue HST and (1) Gold/White HST.

2 Sew together (2) 3½" (8.9cm) Dark Blue squares and (2) 3½" (8.9cm) White squares to form a Four Patch unit. Make 2 units.

3 Sew together (2) Four Patch units and (2) HST to form a block.

4 Repeat steps 1–3 to make (1) Yellow/Green HST, (1) White/Teal HST, and (2) Dark Blue/White Four Patch units. Sew the units together to make a second block.

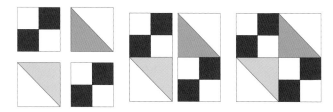

COMPLETING THE QUILT TOP
Prepare the Side-setting Triangles
1 To prepare the side-setting triangles, sew together the triangles (cut from 10" [25.4cm] squares) as shown (1 of each combination):

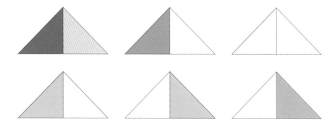

SEW THE BLOCKS AND SETTING TRIANGLES TOGETHER
1 Sew the blocks together in rows, adding the pieced and solid setting triangles as indicated. Note: Since the setting triangles are cut from 10" (25.4cm) squares, they are a little larger than needed, but it is easier to trim the quilt down after completing the center section. Because of the on-point arrangement, the exact measurement (in this case 8.83" [22.4cm]) doesn't leave any room for error.

2 After sewing the blocks and rows together, trim the quilt as needed—**be sure to include a ¼" (6mm) seam allowance** beyond the points of the Star blocks to add the border.

BORDERS
See Measuring for Borders on page 15. Because the blocks are set on point, the border sizes are approximate. It is especially important that you measure through the center to determine the border size. Be careful not to stretch as you measure—there are a lot of bias edges in the quilt.

1 Sew together 8½" (21.6cm) x WOF strips to form a long strip. From this strip, cut side borders—see note above. Side borders should measure about 8½" x 51½" (21.6cm x 131cm). Add side borders to the quilt top.

2 Measure the quilt top again for the width of the quilt with the side borders on. Cut the top and bottom borders—each should measure about 8½" x 50½" (21.6cm x 128.3cm). Add the borders to the top and bottom of the quilt top.

Quilt Assembly Diagram

FINISHING THE QUILT

1 Give the quilt top a good press. Layer and baste. Quilt as desired—we used an edge-to-edge design.

2 Bind the quilt using 2½" (6.4cm) x WOF strips. Don't forget the label!

Border Assembly Diagram

Eat Your Vegetables!

The star block works well with scraps—just use whatever background fabric you have and mix up the star points and centers!

BLOCK 1

For each block, you will need:

- **A** (6) 3½" (8.9cm) squares
- **B** (2) 3½" x 6½" (8.9cm x 16.5cm) rectangles
- **C** (1) 4½" (11.4cm) square cut twice on the diagonal
- **D** (1) 4½" (11.4cm) square cut twice on the diagonal
- **E** (2) 3½" (8.9cm) squares
- **F** (2) 4½" (11.4cm) squares, cut twice on the diagonal

BLOCK 2

For each block, you will need:

- **A** (4) 3½" (8.9cm) squares White
- **B** (4) 3½" (8.9cm) squares Dark Blue
- **C** (1) 7" (17.8cm) square White
- **D** (1) 7" (17.8cm) square Gold
- **E** (1) 7" (17.8cm) square Medium Blue
- **F** (1) 7" (17.8cm) square Coral

BLOCK 1

BLOCK 2

*Made by Daria Eisen, Arlington, VA. Quilted by Deborah G. Stanley, Matawan, NJ
Daria's version of this quilt includes lots of prints from her stash in shades of
olive and celery, along with some black and white for a little extra snap!*

About the Authors

Linda J. Hahn is a multiple award-winning author of nine books! She is a guest designer for Banyan Batiks (Northcott) and is currently working on her third collection. Linda is an EQ Artist and a Janome Maker. She has had over 50 designs and articles published in your favorite quilting magazines, and recently joined the show team at Road to California.

Linda is a high-energy/low-stress instructor. She enjoys taking a complex-looking block or technique and breaking it down into easy and manageable steps. Born in Staten Island, New York, Linda has an affinity toward the New York Beauty block and has a lot of fun experimenting with the different ways that the block can be used in quilt designs.

Linda presents in-person and virtual lectures and workshops at quilt guilds, shows and on cruises.

She is also a multi-licensed Zumba instructor.

Deborah G. Stanley is an independent designer whose work has been published in many quilt magazines, including *Love of Quilting*, *Modern Patchwork*, *American Quilter*, and *Quilter's World*. She is the co-author, with Linda J. Hahn, of *New York Beauty Quilts Electrified* (2018, Fox Chapel Publishing) and *Rock that Quilt Block: Country Crown* (2020, Fox Chapel Publishing). In addition, she has provided many quilting and sewing projects for fabric companies, including Banyan Batiks, Northcott Silk, and Elizabeth's Studio, specializing in simple, easy-to-sew lap quilts and handbags. Deb lives in New Jersey with her husband, Steve. When not quilting, she enjoys reading and crafts of all kinds.

Index